Perspectives of America's Military and Veteran Caregivers

A QUALITATIVE EXPLORATION

PRIYA GANDHI | KAYLA M. WILLIAMS | RAJEEV RAMCHAND

Sponsored by the Elizabeth Dole Foundation

RAND

For more information on this publication, visit **www.rand.org/t/RRA3212-3**.

Published by the RAND Corporation, Santa Monica, Calif.

Library of Congress Cataloging-in-Publication Data is available for this publication.

ISBN: 978-1-9774-1412-0

Cover design by Peter Soriano

Cover photo: Getty Images/adamkaz

About This Report

Released in September 2024, *America's Military and Veteran Caregivers: Hidden Heroes Emerging from the Shadows* (Ramchand et al., 2024), commissioned by the Elizabeth Dole Foundation, presents data from the 2023 RAND Caregiving Survey and produces new estimates of the number of adults caregiving in the United States today; how those caring for wounded, ill, and injured service members and veterans compare with those caring for civilians and with non-caregivers; and the potential impacts of caregiving on caregivers' health, their economic security, and their families' well-being. In this report, RAND researchers present findings from the qualitative arm of this research project, sharing insights gleaned from interviews of, and giving voice to, a subset of America's military and veteran caregivers as they continue their paths emerging from the shadows.

RAND Epstein Family Veterans Policy Research Institute

The RAND Epstein Family Veterans Policy Research Institute is dedicated to conducting innovative, evidence-based research and analysis to improve the lives of those who have served in the U.S. military. Building on decades of interdisciplinary expertise at RAND, the institute prioritizes creative, equitable, and inclusive solutions and interventions that meet the needs of diverse veteran populations while engaging and empowering those who support them. For more information about the RAND Epstein Family Veterans Policy Research Institute, visit veterans.rand.org. Questions about this report or about the RAND Epstein Family Veterans Policy Research Institute should be directed to veteranspolicy@rand.org.

Social and Behavioral Policy Program

RAND Social and Economic Well-Being is a division of RAND that seeks to actively improve the health and social and economic well-being of populations and communities throughout the world. This research was conducted in the Social and Behavioral Policy Program within RAND Social and Economic Well-Being. The program focuses on such topics as risk factors and prevention programs, social safety net programs and other social supports, poverty, aging, disability, child and youth health and well-being, and quality of life, as well as other policy concerns that are influenced by social and behavioral actions and systems that affect wellbeing. For more information, email sbp@rand.org.

Funding

Funding for this research was provided by the Elizabeth Dole Foundation. The researchers benefited from additional support from the Epstein Family Foundation, which established the RAND Epstein Family Veterans Policy Research Institute in 2021.

Acknowledgments

Forty military and veteran caregivers living in the United States today, many of them balancing caring for veterans with their other responsibilities, took time out of their extremely busy schedules not only to respond to the 2023 RAND Caregiving Survey, but also to participate in follow-up interviews. To them, we offer our sincere gratitude. We are also grateful for the insights provided by members of this project's Scientific Advisory Board, who are listed in Table 11.2 of *Emerging from the Shadows* (Ramchand et al., 2024).

We would like to recognize the hard work of NORC at the University of Chicago, especially Martha Crowley, in supporting recruitment efforts, and RAND's Survey Research Group, particularly Danielle Schlang, in carrying out these interviews. Valuable quality assurance reviews were provided by Roxana Delgado and Daniel Siconolfi. We thank Rosa Maria Torres for assistance with generating abbreviations and citations and Nora Spiering for careful editing.

And finally, we thank Elizabeth Dole for her commitment to improving the lives of military and veteran caregivers, and her insistence that this work be informed by research.

Summary

Military and veteran caregivers are *hidden heroes*, a term coined by RAND and the Elizabeth Dole Foundation in 2014 when the organizations partnered to produce *Hidden Heroes: America's Military Caregivers* (Ramchand et al., 2014). That report provided the first ever national portrait of those caring—mostly uncompensated—for wounded, ill, and injured service members and veterans in the United States. *Hidden Heroes* shed light on who was caring for service members and veterans with physical and mental health conditions and elucidated how caregiving affected those caregivers. Subsequent changes, such as expanded programs available to support military and veteran caregivers, the aging of the veteran population, and the coronavirus pandemic, call for new examination of military and veteran caregivers and the services available to support them. *America's Military and Veteran Caregivers: Hidden Heroes Emerging from the Shadows* (Ramchand et al., 2024) provides a new examination of America's hidden heroes by presenting findings from the 2023 RAND Caregiving Survey and the 2022 RAND Veterans Survey. This report supplements that quantitative research with findings from qualitative interviews.

Approach

Thirty-eight qualitative interviews were conducted between December 2023 and February 2024. In their own words, the interviewed military and veteran caregivers provided rich descriptions of their experiences, complementing the survey findings with illustrative anecdotes that deepen our understanding of the challenges and joys of caregiving and elucidate opportunities to improve supportive services.

Key Findings

In discussing their activities, these caregivers highlight aiding care recipients with a broad array of daily tasks that they require, often facing challenges in doing so. These challenges include balancing caregiving with other priorities and commitments; managing care recipients' health-related conditions and needs; financial, emotional, and physical struggles; and difficulty accessing respite and navigating health care systems. Most caregivers reported being able to access at least some of the diverse health care and social services available to support themselves and/or care recipients. Some caregivers mentioned continued unmet needs, often driven by eligibility issues, and facing other obstacles, particularly related to a lack of information regarding services, service accessibility (especially in rural areas), and perceived quality of care. They also noted myriad informal and formal supports they lean on at the individual, interpersonal, institutional, and community levels, most commonly citing support received from family and friends.

Caregivers also discussed their identities, feeling both similar to and different from other caregivers for varying reasons. They felt similar to others based on shared caregiving experiences but noted differences based on achieved characteristics (such as education and employment) rather than ascribed characteristics (such as race and ethnicity or gender identity). Interviewees were mixed in feeling represented by media portrayals of caregivers; some shared that they did not often come across stories that embodied their experiences. Caregivers also discussed interactions with health care professionals, often citing strategies they employed to ensure that they were respected and understood, although some reported experiencing negative interactions.

Caregivers discussed economic impacts they faced, demonstrating a great deal of variability in terms of employment statuses and in whether they were planning for the future or had access to the resources necessary to fulfill future caregiving responsibilities. Even given the diversity of their experiences, caregivers generally stated that their relationships with care recipients had improved over time and said that they found caregiving to be rewarding. Showcasing the positive experiences and challenges they face, caregivers concluded by pointing to opportunities for organizations to improve outreach and provision of services to them—our nation's hidden heroes.

Recommendations

A full set of recommendations for better supporting military and veteran caregivers is provided in *America's Military and Veteran Caregivers: Hidden Heroes Emerging from the Shadows* (Ramchand et al., 2024). We do not make new recommendations in this report; rather, the perspectives of the interviewed caregivers provide additional context for five of the recommendations presented in *Emerging from the Shadows*:

- **Promote work environments that are supportive of caregivers.** Caregivers emphasized the importance of supportive work environments, specifically mentioning telework and the ability to have flexible schedules. Others described engaging in microentrepreneurial enterprises to supplement their incomes.
- **Increase opportunities for caregivers to access available financial support, and offer additional financial compensation to caregivers for the work they perform.** Caregivers not in the workforce described challenges navigating changing financial circumstances and services that might not be available to them because of income-level ineligibility. There are opportunities to provide these caregivers with additional guidance to inform financial and other planning efforts.
- **Encourage health care systems to better integrate caregivers into health care teams.** Caregivers appreciated being included by the health care providers caring for care recipients. However, some caregivers said that they primarily felt respected and understood

because of their own background in health care and knowledge of medical terms or health systems.

- **Focus programmatic and social support within the context of local conditions in which military/veteran caregivers live.** Caregivers noted transportation and other access barriers that increase the time they need to spend caregiving or that increase challenges related to caregiving, demonstrating that virtual resources may be beneficial.
- **Tailor caregiver support programs to reflect caregivers' diverse preferences and needs.** Caregivers often relied on informal support systems and provided suggestions about how formal programs could attract more caregivers. These suggestions included increasing the visibility of diverse and representative caregivers and their stories, creating partnerships with organizations that are likely already serving caregivers (e.g., those serving older adults or religious organizations), and fostering improved access to case managers.

Contents

Figure and Tables

Figure

Tables

CHAPTER 1

Introduction

America's Military and Veteran Caregivers: Hidden Heroes Emerging from the Shadows (Ramchand et al., 2024), commissioned by the Elizabeth Dole Foundation, presents data from the 2023 RAND Caregiving Survey and produces new estimates of the number of adults caregiving in the United States today; how those caring for wounded, ill, and injured service members and veterans compare with those caring for civilians and with non-caregivers; and the potential impacts of caregiving on caregivers' health, their economic security, and their families' well-being. More information on the overall study is presented in Appendix A.

To supplement those quantitative findings, RAND researchers also conducted qualitative interviews with a subset of military and veteran caregivers who agreed to be interviewed. This effort gives voice to a group that is often overlooked and underrecognized, America's military and veteran caregivers. The goal of this research is to hear from caregivers themselves, adding context and richness to the survey findings in their own words. Unlike the survey, interview respondents were not meant to be a representative sample; findings should not be interpreted as such. Rather, the supplementary research described in this report is intended to enrich understandings of caregivers' journeys by highlighting an array of personal experiences.

Methodological Approach

In consultation with the main study's Scientific Advisory Board (see Table 11.2 in Ramchand et al., 2024), we identified several subpopulations of interest (e.g., male caregivers, racial and ethnic minority caregivers or veterans) from the 2023 RAND Caregiving Survey for further in-depth analysis. The survey vendor, NORC at the University of Chicago (hereafter, NORC), sent a follow-up survey to 295 military and veteran caregivers asking whether they were willing to be contacted to participate in qualitative interviews. RAND's Survey Research Group (SRG) contacted 90 of those who agreed. Of those, 32 did not respond, 11 were deemed ineligible, and seven canceled or did not show up for interviews. SRG completed interviews with 40 individuals. Coders later decided to exclude two of those who appeared to be paid caregivers, resulting in a final sample of 38.

Interviews consisted of systematic but open-ended questions about caregivers' and care recipients' needs and the resources to support them, experiences with health care teams, the impacts of caregiving, and how relationships are affected by caregiving. The interview protocol is provided in Appendix B.

Additional information about the methodology for selecting, recruiting, and interviewing respondents, as well as the coding of interview transcripts and thematic analysis, is presented in Appendix A. This report presents the themes gleaned from the interviews using terminology from the protocol and caregivers, where possible, to best elevate caregivers' voices and experiences.

Organization of This Report

This report is divided into nine chapters. In Chapter 2, we describe the sample of 38 caregivers who participated in the interviews. In Chapters 3 through 8, we describe what caregivers told us about their needs; their perspectives on the supports available to them; their perceptions of caregiving identities, portrayals, and experiences; the economic impacts of caregiving; their relationships with care recipients; and their suggestions for improvements. These chapters align with the thematic grouping of questions from the interview protocol (see Appendix A). In Chapter 9, we conclude and offer additional context for five recommendations provided in *Emerging from the Shadows* (Ramchand et al., 2024).

Study Limitations and Caveats

Although this report offers important insights in military and veteran caregivers' own words to help ground the survey findings, the nature of this qualitative research necessitates consideration of limitations. The themes reported here are not generalizable. Rather, they represent the voices of a nonrepresentative subset of military and veteran caregivers, shedding light on their diverse day-to-day experiences. Furthermore, while the researchers hoped to probe this element of the intersection of identity and caregiving, the subgroups intentionally sampled in this research (including those who identify as Black or lesbian, gay, bisexual, transgender, queer, or other sexual and gender minority [LGBTQ+] caregivers) often did not raise their ascribed identities when discussing their experiences. Chapter 3 offers more detail into the role of achieved versus ascribed characteristics for those caregivers we interviewed.

CHAPTER 2

Sample Characteristics

Of the 38 military and veteran caregiver interviewees who were identified through the 2023 RAND Caregiving Survey, 28 reported that the care recipient met the RAND construct for catastrophic injury;[1] 20 reported caring for a veteran with a mental health condition; 28 believed that their care recipient's physical or mental health condition (hereafter referred to as *health-related condition*) may have resulted from toxic exposure during their military service (e.g., burn pits, Agent Orange, other toxic substances); and 16 reported caring for someone with a neurological condition such as Alzheimer's disease or other dementia, spinal cord injury, or stroke. According to their survey responses, these interviewees included eight individuals identifying as men, six identifying as LGBTQ+, eight identifying as Black, seven identifying as Hispanic, and five who were themselves veterans.

Twenty-nine caregivers provided care for a man, eight provided care for a woman, and one provided care for someone who did not identify as a man or as a woman. Caregivers most commonly reported that the care recipient was a husband (n = 7); others reported that the care recipient was a spouse, a partner, a life partner, someone they had dated, or a boyfriend. The next most reported relationship category was father (n = 6); other caregivers listed the care recipients as stepfather, mother-in-law, and father-in-law. Other relatives being cared for included grandparents (two grandfathers and one grandmother) and an uncle. Two people were caring for their brothers, one was caring for a sister, and one was caring for a brother-in-law. An additional eight people said that they were caring for friends and neighbors.

We chose to exclude two interviewees who appeared to exclusively be providing care in paid capacities. In one additional case, the interviewee referred to the care recipient as a friend but also used the term *client* and referred to caregiving activities as a "job"; in another, the caregiver was a family friend who worked for a home health agency, and the care recipient's family eventually asked whether they would "be interested in coming to work for him

[1] This construct was created by selecting survey respondents who reported that the veteran for whom they provided care needed help with at least one activity of daily living (ADL) *and* had at least one of these conditions: a neurological condition such as Alzheimer's disease or other dementia, spinal cord injury, or stroke; a traumatic brain injury (TBI); or a musculoskeletal disorder, such as osteoarthritis or rheumatoid arthritis, osteoporosis (thinning of the bones), chronic back pain or sciatica, or any amputated hands, arms, feet, or legs *OR* had either posttraumatic stress disorder (PTSD), major depressive disorder, or another mental health condition *AND* needed help coping with stressful situations or avoiding "triggers" of anxiety or antisocial behavior.

full time." These cases indicated that the line between being a paid and unpaid caregiver could be somewhat blurred or may change over time from more-informal to more-formal caregiving relationships, sometimes referred to as *gray market* caregiving. (Shih et al., 2022).

Interviewees reported caring for veterans who served across several military branches: Thirteen had served in the Army, nine had served in the Navy, four had served in the Air Force, one had served in the Navy Reserves, one had served in the Coast Guard, and one had served as a merchant mariner.[2] An additional nine interviewees believed that the care recipient had served in the military but did not know in which branch of service. Care recipients had served in World War II, the Cold War era, the Korean War or the Korean War era, the Vietnam War or the Vietnam War era, and the post-9/11 era (the era after the September 11, 2001, attacks); again, many caregivers were unclear on the specifics. Those who knew care recipients' length of service reported a range from just a few months (for one care recipient who was discharged during basic training after the onset of a seizure disorder) to 30 years.

Caregivers reported a wide array of health-related conditions among care recipients, including TBI, PTSD and other anxiety disorders, depression, alcohol use disorder, stroke, dementia, musculoskeletal conditions, vision or hearing loss, amputations, seizures, migraines, arthritis, diabetes, cancer, spinal cord injuries, heart disease, and sleep apnea. Among interviewees, 14 reported that the health-related conditions were related to service; these conditions included combat-related injuries, such as one TBI caused by a roadside bomb and one from being shot in post-9/11 conflicts; combat-related exposures, such as Agent Orange in Vietnam; a spinal cord injury and an amputation sustained on duty; and service-related musculoskeletal problems, such as back problems believed to be caused by jumping out of airplanes and foot problems linked to marching. Several interviewees reported that care recipients suffered from PTSD, depression, or other issues related to mental health or mood and believed these to be caused by military service. Others reported that care recipients' health-related conditions were not connected to their military service, including several conditions linked to aging, such as stroke, dementia, physical decline, memory, and mobility issues. In one case, a seizure disorder first manifested during initial entry training and led to early discharge; in another, a preexisting eye injury was believed to be exacerbated by military service. Finally, several interviewees reported that they did not know or were unsure whether the care recipients' injuries or illnesses were related to military service.

How long caregivers had provided or had been providing care varied from less than one year to 20 years. Some interviewees also noted that the level of care changed over time, in several cases becoming progressively more intense as a disease or health-related condition worsened or as the care recipient aged. In one case, the caregiver provided care while her spouse had a severe case of coronavirus disease 2019 (COVID-19), and he has since recovered; in five

---

2 Although merchant mariners are generally not considered veterans and are not fully eligible for federal benefits, some who served during World War II are eligible for all veterans' benefits (see Szymendera, 2017). Because this interviewee's father had served in that era, we chose to include this interview in the final sample.

cases, the caregiver identified in the survey was no longer providing care because the care recipient had since died. Interviews were conducted from December 2023 through February 2024, approximately nine months after the 2023 RAND Caregiver Survey closed.

CHAPTER 3

Caregiver Activities, Challenges, and Service Utilization

The nature of caregiving is not monolithic, given the diversity of health-related conditions and needs of care recipients. As described in *Emerging from the Shadows*, many military and veteran care recipients have chronic conditions, such as cardiovascular conditions, but also prevalent are mental health conditions, hearing problems, and musculoskeletal disorders (Ramchand et al., 2024). This chapter will discuss the types of support needed by care recipients given such conditions, challenges facing caregivers, services that caregivers and care recipients are unable to access and related barriers, and whether and how caregivers receive support in their roles.

Many Caregivers Assisted with Activities of Daily Living, and Almost All Assisted with Instrumental Activities of Daily Living

Care recipients' needs and abilities to function are often characterized by ADLs and instrumental activities of daily living (IADLs). ADLs include eating, bathing, using the toilet, dressing, and mobility. Over half of military and veteran caregivers help with at least one ADL (Ramchand et al., 2024). IADLs are tasks that enable individuals to live independently, including household errands and tasks, food preparation, managing finances, and transportation (U.S. Department of Veterans Affairs, 2023).

Several caregivers reported during the interviews that they provided assistance with ADLs, and their description of performing these tasks described their level of involvement:

> Basically everything. I have to do the house. I have to help him get a shower, get his shoes on, his pants. He puts his shirt on, but I have to help him with his pants, and I make his bed, do the dishes, stuff like that. I transport him to the store. I go to the store for him.
>
> —Partner caregiver of Army veteran

> And so he just couldn't use that right hand anymore. Things like dressing and eating and everything just became much, much more complicated. . . . But at that point, when it came

> down to meals and bathing and dressing, those kinds of things that he could not do with one hand, I quit my full-time banking job.
>
> —Adult child caregiver of World War II Merchant Marine veteran

On the other hand, almost all caregivers, including almost all of those who helped with ADLs, provided assistance with IADLs. While some caregivers minimized the burden of these activities relative to ADLs, their descriptions of assisting with these tasks also demonstrate the length of time they can take:

> I mean, he's very self-sufficient. But I prepare meals and run his errands, grocery shopping and that kind of thing. And take care of the house, keep it up for him. . . . I would say keeping things clean, fixing broken things, preparing meals, and also, again, running errands. . . . But I don't need to, at this point at least, help him do any personal hygiene, upkeep, or anything like that. He can still do all of that.
>
> —Adult child caregiver of Navy Reserves veteran

> His yard, cleaning, getting his food ready when he had to—I delivered it, I did packages for him. What else can I do for him? I did all his bills. I did all of everything. He couldn't write very well, and I made sure that his electronics were all working fine.
>
> —Sibling caregiver of Coast Guard veteran

A key finding in *Emerging from the Shadows* is that caregiving activities for someone with serious mental health conditions may not be adequately captured in standard measures of caregiving (Ramchand et al., 2024). One caregiver relayed what some of these activities entail:

> Here at home I have to have all his medications locked up in a safe, because he has tried to take his life before, and one of the things he has done that with is medications. . . . My biggest challenge is to make sure that he doesn't try to take his own life again.
>
> —Spouse caregiver of post-9/11-era Army veteran

Caregivers Face an Array of Challenges Associated with Caregiving

Emerging from the Shadows (Ramchand et al., 2024) presents information on such constructs as *caregiver burden*, which provides a standardized empirical measure that helps quantify challenges that caregivers face in providing care. These interviews provided caregivers with the opportunity to describe these challenges in their own terms. When initially asked about the most significant challenges they faced in their roles, caregivers spoke about the following: balancing time commitments, how care recipients' health-related conditions dictated the most challenging caregiving needs, financial challenges associated with caregiving, emotional challenges associated with caregiving, physical challenges associated with caregiving, difficulty obtaining respite, and difficulty navigating the health care system. These categories are discussed in the following sections and further elucidated in other chapters of this report, particularly as related to caregivers' perceptions of supports available to them (Chapter 4) and of the economic impacts of caregiving (Chapter 6).

Balancing Time Commitments Can Be Difficult

Several caregivers discussed the difficulty in balancing their time commitments (such as professional employment and personal and parental responsibilities) because of their caregiving responsibilities. In fact, approximately 40 percent of all military and veteran caregivers are also caring for a child under age 18 (Ramchand et al., 2024), and the caregivers we interviewed specifically noted challenges balancing their caregiving duties with other family responsibilities:

> I think it's really—one is I have my own family. So it's a balance and finding the time to help him because he's my parent. So I need to find the time to help him, but also finding the time for my own family.
>
> —Adult child caregiver of Cold War–era Army veteran

> Not being able to do side work, and I have children too, not being able to give them my full attention. Like, I have to have my own doctor's appointment, and I don't have time for myself.
>
> —Adult grandchild caregiver of Air Force veteran

Care Recipients' Health-Related Conditions and Related Needs Cause Challenges

Caregivers emphasized the challenges that can stem from the acuity and severity of care recipients' health-related conditions and related needs. A few further described how care recipients can be hesitant to receive support or resistant to engaging in helpful activities (e.g., leaving the home).

> He doesn't see that he needs the care, that he really resists it sometimes, and I have to convince him. And I think that sometimes I have to almost play a game with him to get him to understand that he needs the care, or I have to tell him that our mother said he needs to do it and then he will.
>
> —Sibling caregiver of Cold War–era veteran, unspecified service

> Just for instance, with him being sick last week, he was in a lot of pain, and he had no control of his bowel movements, and that was a big challenge for me, because I've never

> experienced that until last week. I had to help him out of the bed. I had to help him to the shower, and he's got one of them sit-down-like showers where he can sit and shower. He gave himself a shower. Basically, I had to make sure that he didn't try to get up and walk, make sure he was eating, drinking, taking his medication. It's a job.
>
> —Adult child caregiver of Vietnam Navy veteran

Caregiving Can Create a Financial Burden

Emerging from the Shadows estimates that military and veteran caregivers spend approximately $8,500 annually in out-of-pocket costs associated with caregiving (Ramchand et al., 2024). Some caregivers highlighted financial considerations and challenges they and care recipients faced regarding such costs:

> So, and financial, it's devastating; like, we're waiting on the back pay from his disability case, but we've got a mountain of medical debt. Absolute, like all I do is juggle bills all the time to try to make ends meet and then we've got co-pays for the doctor, we've got co-pays for the medication. If there's specialists he has to see, sometimes insurance won't cover it. So we have to pay out of pocket; sometimes the insurance denies medication, and so we've got to pay out of pocket for it until they decide if they do want to cover it. I have to purchase a tremendous amount of over-the-counter medications for him as well out of pocket. Because of the vomiting from the migraine and stuff like that, like his teeth are all messed up. So there's a huge dental bill even though we have dental insurance. And then sometimes, like I gave in a couple of years ago and actually started hiring someone to help, once a week to come in and do chores like, do the laundry, cleaning, stuff like that because I couldn't, I just couldn't handle it anymore. And so that's expensive too, and I got to pay the person to help out around here; it gives me a little bit of sanity to have at least someone come in and do some of the stuff so that I don't have to.
>
> —Partner caregiver of post-9/11-era Navy veteran

Increased costs associated with caregiving may contribute to financial stressors that military and veteran caregivers face. Forty-eight percent of military and veteran caregivers to those over 60 years of age, and 70 percent of caregivers to those 60 years of age and under, report difficulty paying bills (Ramchand et al., 2024). For some caregivers, financial challenges are even more stressful than caregiving per se, as exemplified in the following quote:

> It's financial challenges, because sometimes there's things that stress my dad out per se. If an extra bill comes along and we don't have the money to pay it right away. Basically, I mean, I feel as, him being a disabled veteran, his pay that he gets every month, I don't see how people survive off of that.
>
> —Adult child caregiver of Vietnam Navy veteran

Emotional Burdens Can Be Substantial

A wealth of empirical literature documents the emotional stress of caregiving. Among those caring for service members or veterans 60 years of age or under, 75 percent met criteria for high levels of perceived stress, and 43 percent met criteria for depression (Ramchand et al., 2024).[1] During the interviews, caregivers discussed the emotional burden they faced, often using the terms *stressed* and *overwhelmed* to describe their feelings.

> Emotionally, I'm, a lot of times—I'm very frustrated. I'm tired all the time. It's really hard for me to have the energy to do the things that I want to do because I'm always taking care of him. We don't go out; we don't do anything, like—we're home most of the time. And then he gets really frustrated with his situation and he gets depressed, and he talks about, like, "I can't live like this, and this is too much for me to deal with," and then I have to be like, "You need to be strong for me, I can't carry us both emotionally through this, I know it's really tough and it's frustrating." And he's like, "I don't want to live like this anymore."
>
> —Partner caregiver of post-9/11-era Navy veteran

> Just the typical, sometimes you feel you're a little bit overwhelmed and you're by yourself doing everything.
>
> —Family member caregiver of Vietnam Navy veteran

Notably, the emotional strain of caregiving is not eliminated if the care recipient's health-related condition worsens to a degree that causes them to require institutional care:

> For me, I'm still a little in limbo because I'm still a wife, but I'm not a wife and I'm not a widow. I have some level of freedom that I didn't have before, but I don't now . . . . even though they are no longer at home, we are still caregivers. And in some ways, having them reach the point that they have to be in care, the caregiving actually becomes more difficult . . . you have to learn how to give up control. . . . Going to visit them, one never knows what one is going to find when they go in. Is he going to be asleep? Is he going to be awake? Is he going to be pleasant? Is he going to be unpleasant? Is he happy to see you? Is he going to be asking you continuously, "When am I coming home?" It's the complete unknown of what you're going to face when you get over there.
>
> —Spouse caregiver of Vietnam Air Force veteran

Physical Burdens Challenge Some Caregivers

Between 55 and 60 percent of military and veteran caregivers report at least one physical limitation, more so than non-caregivers (Ramchand et al., 2024). A few caregivers we interviewed highlighted the physical burdens of supporting care recipients that may contribute to or are

---

[1] Among military and veteran caregivers to those over 60 years of age, 44 percent met criteria for high perceived stress, and 15 percent met criteria for depression (Ramchand et al., 2024).

compounded by caregivers' own health-related conditions or limitations. These descriptions often involved caring for those who were physically larger than them:

> His size, if that makes sense. . . . Yes, he's like 6'3" and like 300 pounds. So, it can be, sometimes it can be difficult to help him out if he really needs help getting in the shower or whatever.
>
> —Brother-in-law caregiver of post-9/11-era Navy veteran

> He's pretty tall. He's almost 6' and I'm 5'4", so that's an issue right there. He's thinner so that's helpful, but just to help him sometimes, like, especially the tub, that's kind of a struggle because he's so long, his legs are so long. So, just the logistics of it, it's hard, and it's hard on my back, and I have back issues from it over the years, and he has issues with his arms because he's using his arms so much to lift himself, and he's stubborn-headed sometimes and he wants to do it all himself.
>
> —Partner caregiver of post-9/11-era Navy veteran

Difficulty in Gaining Respite Causes Strain

A few caregivers relatedly discussed the difficulty in gaining respite from their responsibilities, using the term *respite* generally and not specific to receiving formal respite services. Around 40 percent of military and veteran caregivers reported that for them, it was very or somewhat difficult to obtain task support to "take a break" (Ramchand et al., 2024). These interviews revealed that many caregivers do not want respite only from caregiving, but often also from additional personal or professional responsibilities:

> The respite I'd say [resonates as a challenge] a little bit. There are some days where I'm like, "Man, I don't wanna do anything today. I've been on go all week. I'd rather not go over there [to the care recipient's house], but I've got to go over there anyway." Again, I don't go over there every day. I'd say it's more like an every other day situation. So, I am getting breaks from it.
>
> —Nephew caregiver of Cold War–era Navy veteran

> I gave up my life. Like I said, I was a 30-year banker. My husband and I had been married several years. We would go on vacations and do things. When I became my dad's caregiver, I basically was under house arrest. I was there 24/7, 365, with very little break.
>
> —Adult child caregiver of World War II Merchant Marine veteran

Healthcare Systems Can Be Difficult to Navigate

Emerging from the Shadows provides caregivers' descriptions of how well they feel integrated into care recipients' health care teams. Only one-third, for example, felt listened to or that health care providers sought their input. Perhaps more striking, nearly one-third of caregivers also reported experiencing hassles in health care, such as reminding health care staff to do things for the care recipient or experiencing delays in completing paperwork (Ramchand et al., 2024). During these interviews, a few caregivers discussed in more detail challenges they faced in navigating the health care system, particularly with accessing benefits and adequate health care for care recipients:

> So yeah, the doctors, it's a constant. I spend so many hours every week dealing with the doctors getting preauthorizations taken care of, making sure the medication gets filled on time, making sure the doctors write the prescription, making sure the insurance covers the prescription, fighting with the insurance company, booking appointments, scheduling. Those are the biggest challenges, and then finding doctors who are willing to work with us, because doctors don't like a case where it's like, "I can't fix you; it's a chronic condition that's ongoing." And so they start to get frustrated and burnt out because it's just an onslaught of medications all the time. . . . You don't know how many doctors we go through all the time. They're just like, "I don't want to deal with it anymore, go find another doctor." So that's one aspect of it is the medical advocacy and taking care of all the medical stuff.
>
> —Partner caregiver of post-9/11-era Navy veteran

> The caregiver place that we hired was wonderful, and they figured out that they could go through the VA [U.S. Department of Veterans Affairs] to get paid. So, it took over a year to get all of that paperwork put together, but we finally got it. So now a caregiver comes twice a week I think, other than me, and the VA pays for that. . . . So, I guess, my challenge was that (a) we didn't know about any of these benefits and even still, we're finding out slowly more and more benefits that she can access and (b) the loops that you have to jump through in order to get these benefits is astronomical. It's gotten a lot better, and I know that the federal government is working to try and help our veterans more, but certainly in the very beginning, it was almost impossible to get anything.
>
> —Sibling caregiver of Army veteran

Access to Services for Caregivers and Care Recipients Varied Widely

Emerging from the Shadows (Ramchand et al., 2024) describes caregivers' access to programs and services for themselves but did not focus on barriers they faced accessing services for care recipients. For this reason, in these interviews, we asked caregivers whether they were able to access necessary health care and other support services for care recipients; most agreed that they could. However, some still noted that they had unmet needs, and others described difficulties accessing available services.

Some Found Many Available Services

Caregivers cited benefits afforded by health insurance plans, including private health insurance and coverage offered by VA:

> I mean, VA, I think he mostly went, there was a clinic in [location] he went to sometimes and then a hospital in, I want to say [different location] . . . . And they had fairly regular care and so forth. All of his prescriptions mostly came through the VA mail order clinic. A couple of them, he had to have filled here in town. There's no problem. I can't think of any real major issues.
>
> —Adult child caregiver of Korean War Army veteran

> No, matter of fact, I never saw so many benefits in my life. He had everything.
>
> —Sibling caregiver of Coast Guard veteran

Among these caregivers, a few noted the adequacy of these benefits being correlated to their care recipients' health-related conditions being of lesser acuity and severity; one caregiver further described the general availability of health and social services:

> Again, he doesn't need any physical services or assistance at this point. But if it comes down to that, again, our greater community here has sufficient resources. For example, when my mother was ill, we were able to have oxygen for her and nurses that would come in once or twice a week to check on her and take care of her. And so, there are services like that that are really good and easily scheduled.
>
> —Adult child caregiver of Navy Reserves veteran

A few caregivers also emphasized receiving responsive care that met emergent needs. One caregiver shared:

> He became very weak and couldn't even hardly stand. And then at that point, I thought, this is it. He's dying. There's no way this 95-year-old is going to survive COVID. But sure enough he did. However, at that point, I had called in to his doctor here in [state], and they put him on hospice care. So, I did get some help from the hospice people. They were able to come and help with the bathing part of it and some of those other things that hospice does. . . . Very easy. And I'd have to say immediate. I mean, I made a call to the doctor's office, and it was like the same day that hospice showed up with supplies and things. It was truly amazing.
>
> —Adult child caregiver of World War II Merchant Marine veteran

Other Caregivers Had Unmet Needs

Yet, some caregivers reflected on services that they and care recipients needed but were unable to access, in part because they had been told that they were ineligible. These include health care services (e.g., case management), more and higher-quality medical equipment and supplies (e.g., a walker), and trainings and education for caregivers to support their caregiving (e.g., cardiopulmonary resuscitation and nursing classes).

One caregiver shared the difficulty associated with not meeting the disability thresholds needed to qualify for services:

> So I've asked for a case manager for years, and he's not sick enough for a case manager. Like he's got to be on death's door, I guess, [for] a case manager—because it's so much work to manage all this, the medical aspect of it. And so I'm like, if I have a case manager, they could coordinate the care and take some of the burden off of me, and they just [say], like, "We're sorry, but he's not that sick according to us." And then it's fighting with the insurance company and the doctors.
>
> —Partner caregiver of post-9/11-era Navy veteran

A common barrier to services was a lack of adequate health care coverage, often because of issues qualifying for specific benefits given caregivers' and care recipients' income levels and occasionally because of age eligibility thresholds.

> He's not on Medicare or Medicaid because he's not old enough. So, there's really no things that can help him. No medical services, he's on [health plan] for medical. But, I mean, as far as somebody coming over and taking over for me and cleaning for him and, helping with that and stuff like that, there isn't any because you don't have the medical coverage for that.
>
> —Partner caregiver of Army veteran

> Well, he's tried to get on the VA, but they say with mine and his, both Social Security, we make too much money. I'm thinking he tried maybe three years ago, but he had tried several years prior to that also. So, he's tried it twice.
>
> —Spouse caregiver of Air Force veteran

Caregivers May Face Other Difficulties Related to Accessing Services

Across caregivers who stated that they could or could not access services, some highlighted the lengthy processes involved in accessing health care benefits for care recipients, often requiring caregivers to intervene and advocate:

> I mean, a lot of times things are more of a process, but, I mean, I spent my adult career in health care. I know this and I understand it, and I don't get—you know, I talk to other people, and they were just so angry that you got to do this, you got to do that. And that's

just health care. I mean, if I wanted to have something done, my insurance company isn't going to automatically pay for it either.

—Spouse caregiver of Vietnam veteran, unspecified service

The transition from, because he's been getting veterans benefits and like health care for a very long time. Transitioning there from [state] to [state] was hard because no one was answering the phone, no one actually wanted to talk to you and give you the right information. The resources just seem very scattered, changing. Just to make sure he was up to date, just to make sure they knew new addresses and they knew any new information. Contacting someone was very hard. It was a lot of emails back and forth. A lot of miscommunication to the point that when we got up there, we just like went to the actual office and that was like hours of waiting and waiting to properly handle everything.

—Adult grandchild caregiver of Army veteran

A few caregivers also discussed experiences in which care recipients received health care services that lacked "quality" or cultural sensitivity.

It's the quality of care. Even though he's had a TBI, even though all his blood work has come back—for the past two, three years, his hematocrit levels were bad. This was wrong, that was wrong. Now his thyroid is messed up. And this all stems from that pituitary gland due to the traumatic brain injury, and they've never done anything. He has had to go through all this, and he finally saw a good doctor last month and was like, "Look at my levels. I've been on testosterone. This level is wrong, that level is wrong. My thyroid levels are wrong." And the doctor finally said, "Oh, okay, we'll get you somebody." But you have to fight and nag for every inch, it seems like, with this veteran health care.

—Spouse caregiver of post-9/11-era Army veteran

Well, the mental health, I mean, the, the VA's answer to her need for a therapist is to put her in a room with a bunch of men and have a group talk. Well, her PTSD is from being raped, so she can't sit in a room full of men and talk about it. So, yeah, the VA needs to work on their mental health services.

—Sibling caregiver of Army veteran

Only one caregiver discussed using respite care services, although a few mentioned experiencing caregiving burdens, potentially demonstrating the utility of such services:

I mean, we did use the respite care that is part of the hospice. There was five days in January of 2022, the year that he died, that I had kind of become at the end of my rope. It was getting much, much harder and I needed a break, and they told me that there is the respite care that's available through hospice. And so he went to stay in a nursing home for five days and then it was very—it wasn't what I thought it was going to be. It was very challenging for me. I don't think it was great for him. He came back from there very medi-

> cated, where he didn't go there medicated, but he came back very medicated. But so, it was a big challenge.
>
> —Adult child caregiver of World War II Merchant Marine veteran

> Getting respite can be hard just because it's not really a service a lot of people provide, but we try to give each other respite and, like I said, during the day, and we have no time.
>
> —Brother-in-law caregiver of post-9/11-era Navy veteran

Many Caregivers Faced Obstacles Accessing Services

In a separate section of the protocol, the RAND team asked caregivers about specific obstacles they encountered in accessing the services they shared as being necessary for them and care recipients. In their responses, caregivers discussed the lack of information about caregiver services, geographical barriers, and process challenges.

Lack of Information Was Frequently Mentioned

The most commonly discussed obstacles were a lack of adequate information, particularly related to accessing benefits, and communication issues.

> At the time, I might have liked it, more support when it came to trying to figure out what to do next with his care and figuring out medically where we should go because there was problems trying to pinpoint what his diagnosis was. So I could have used some help, figure out where to take him.
>
> —Spouse caregiver of Vietnam Army veteran

> Well, sometimes they don't communicate with the right person, and they tell you, like, evasions, they pass you to another person, who gives you an answer, and a lot of waiting time on the phone. Sometimes you have to cancel things or things don't go accordingly. A lot of paperwork.
>
> —Friend caregiver of veteran, unspecified service

Rural Caregivers Experienced Geographic Barriers

A few caregivers also described geographic barriers to care, such as longer distances to access care or a shortage of options in rural areas.

> She was going to the VA clinic down here, but they closed and they're about just as worse. Communication-wise and appointment times, which I know a lot of the veterans they need to get in, but they need to expand or get more doctors. The one down here, the one that's close to us that we are able to go to, they have closed that location. [The

> other location], it's in [city], which is about 45 minutes to an hour away. I won't be able to commit to making the drive every time.
>
> —Adult grandchild caregiver of Air Force veteran

> I mean, this is a fairly rural area, so medical transportation and so forth can be tricky. But between [my sister] and I, we always managed to do that.
>
> —Adult child caregiver of Korean War Army veteran

> [Question from interviewer: Do you feel that there are support systems or groups available for you personally?] Not in my area. We live in a rural area. So now because if there was, I would definitely take them up on it.
>
> —Friend caregiver of post-9/11-era Navy veteran

Although these statements suggest that caregivers in rural environments may encounter specific barriers to care, it is worth noting that in *Emerging from the Shadows* service utilization between military and veteran caregivers in rural areas did not differ from that of those in more urban environments (Ramchand et al., 2024).

Lengthy Processes Posed a Barrier

A couple of caregivers also discussed lengthy processes associated with navigating bureaucracies being obstacles.

> I was put in touch with a social worker. The social worker would go down to travel pay, talk to travel pay, travel pay would have issues. So then she would go to Department of Health and Human Services, but it's through the VA and they would give us $10 gas cards and they would give us three of the $10 gas cards to try to at least help us. . . . Right now, they're two months behind. They're starting to catch up a little bit, but that's our biggest pet peeve because it costs about $120 in gas to go to and from, and by doing that, that takes away from either an electric bill or something like that.
>
> —Friend caregiver of post-9/11-era Navy veteran

> [W]e had to first follow the proper departments for support, and then we had to go through the approval process, and due to her debilitation, she could not do a lot of these things on her own. So, my wife had to assume power of attorney to make decisions for her, and so that was another process that took some time.
>
> —Son-in-law caregiver of Army veteran

Other obstacles included poor experiences with in-home caregiving services, a perceived lack of health care providers trusting caregivers, and inadequate funds; these are described in subsequent chapters.

CHAPTER 4

Supports Available to Caregivers

Emerging from the Shadows sheds light on the programs and services that military and veteran caregivers used, from mental health care and routine medical checkups to services designed specifically for caregivers, such as trainings, support groups, and respite care. Many military and veteran caregivers access these programs; a greater proportion of those caring for service members and veterans 60 years of age and under used these services relative to those caring for those over 60 years of age. However, military and veterans did suggest additional services they wanted, including services they could do with the care recipient, services that kept care recipients safe at home, and services that reduced caregiver stress (Ramchand et al., 2024).

These interviews probed more directly about caregivers' use of support services. When asked to describe whether and which supports were available to them to assist in carrying out their caregiving responsibilities, caregivers described how they accessed informal and formal support (hereafter, broadly referred to as *support*) from family and friends, community organizations, support groups, and health and social services, including VA. Some also described their rationale for not using supports.

Family and Friends Were the Most Commonly Mentioned Sources of Support

One-third of military and veteran caregivers to those over 60 years of age and half of military and veteran caregivers to those 60 years of age and under are *sole caregivers*, meaning that they reported having nobody in their support network (Ramchand et al., 2024). When asked directly about their sources of support in these interviews, caregivers identified family and friends as the most common source of support by providing assistance to caregivers (for instance, stepping in when caregivers have other time-sensitive responsibilities and offering emotional support) and to care recipients (for instance, providing social comfort and activities).

> Professional services, no. But in terms of support from family, absolutely. There's family members that will help cook, that will help watch her, or be with her, or take her to enjoy time outside or see other family members.
>
> —Son-in-law caregiver of Army veteran

> I receive some from my other family members if they have the time. Sometimes I get help from my friends. . . . Like with transportation if I need that. If I need some money that I don't have at the time, they'll lend that to me and then I'll pay back when I can.
>
> —Adult grandchild caregiver of veteran, unspecified service

Community Organizations Were Mentioned as Providing Support

Some caregivers identified community organizations and social services through which they have been able to access informal and formal supports particularly for care recipients. In *Emerging from the Shadows*, 53 percent of military and veteran caregivers reported using home health services (Ramchand et al., 2024). In these interviews, a caregiver reported home-based health services as being particularly supportive:

> The Hospital at Home was a big help, and I don't think we had anybody else come in. Somebody came every day. The first four or five days, I think a doctor called. They loaned [the care recipient] . . . a tablet, and the doctor would call that—they had FaceTime on the tablet. And then after that, it was just medication delivery or blood samples that [were] picked up, and then a nurse was always available 24 hours a day by phone.
>
> —Spouse caregiver of Vietnam veteran, unspecified service

Another spoke of a community-based service that provided respite outside of the home as being beneficial:

> There's one place that is called [community organization]. They help with them, they have some volunteer people that come like mentors, and they come, and they pick them up and they take them to the coffee shop and things like that.
>
> —Friend caregiver of Air Force veteran

Some Caregivers Used Formal and Less Formal Support Groups

Among military and veteran caregivers to those 60 years of age and under, 30 percent used an in-person support group and 15 percent had accessed an online support group; among military and veteran caregivers to those over 60 years of age, 10 percent used an in-person group and 8 percent used an online group (Ramchand et al., 2024). Some caregivers specifically discussed the role of caregiver support groups (both in person and virtually) in providing emotional support and respite from their responsibilities.

> There's something on Facebook that I'm a part of that, you know, other people that are in that position in the area, or people who are in-home CNAs [certified nursing assistants], or whatever, always post things. So, I guess that would be considered a support group there.
>
> —Neighbor caregiver of Army veteran

One caregiver mentioned specifically that in addition to a support group, their church offers "congregation":

> Yes, since the summer there's a group of caregivers who meet once a month by telephone and give classes, and you know the classes by heart, but anyway. There's that, and I congregate in a church.
>
> —Spouse caregiver of post-9/11-era Army veteran

Relatedly, 14 percent of those who used an in-person support group met at a "church, synagogue, mosque, or other religious organization," suggesting the importance of faith-based communities in supporting military and veteran caregivers (Ramchand et al., 2024).

Some caregivers highlighted more-informal support they received from other caregivers and online resources.

> Yes, but basically sometimes it's a support group, like caregivers. We share information, experiences, opinions.
>
> —Friend caregiver of veteran, unspecified service

> When you go online, there's a couple of websites where you can get more information about what you can do and different ideas that you can help out with.
>
> —Adult grandchild caregiver of veteran, unspecified service

Some Caregivers Specifically Appreciated VA-Provided Supports

VA is an important source of health care (though not the sole source) for veteran care recipients and their caregivers. In fact, 35 percent of care recipients receive most of their care from VA (Ramchand et al., 2024). It is not surprising, then, that some caregivers also mentioned nonspecific covered health care benefits, often through VA, as important mechanisms of informal and formal support.

> The VA lady, yes, the VA lady. She helps facilitate doctor's appointment[s] or getting him, like if I couldn't do it. She helped him with balancing his checkbook. You know, those kind of things, beneficial for him, but nothing as far as the caretaker role would go.
>
> —Neighbor caregiver of Army veteran

> They have the case manager with the insurance. He has worked with us a lot, especially at the beginning and stuff, and now it's all set up on routine. They ship all his catheters and everything to the house, so it makes it easy. That's a huge thing right there. Just sending all his supplies and everything right to the house. It's an automatic shipment so that helps . . . through the VA.
>
> —Partner caregiver of post-9/11-era Navy veteran

Caregivers Did Not Use Formal Supports Because of a Lack of Perceived Need for Them, a Lack of Such Supports, and Ineligibility for Them

Emerging from the Shadows (Ramchand et al., 2024) does not present data on specific barriers to accessing caregiving support. Many caregivers reflected that that they did not need or did not yet need to use formal supports, including some who had used in the past but did not think they were beneficial:

> Yeah, if I wanted them, yeah. And then at the beginning I definitely reached out and so . . . I think we've just adapted through the years so much now that it's routine here.
>
> —Partner caregiver of post-9/11-era Navy veteran

> I know that at the main campus at the hospital they have monthly—they call them drop-in meetings that people can go to as caregivers either to seek support, representation, or respite. I've never felt the need to go to it, but it's there if I would want it.
>
> —Spouse caregiver of Vietnam veteran, unspecified service

> I have in the past [attended a VA support group]. I'm not presently and it's not that I have anything against the organization or the people that are doing it, but it just, it was not something that was really beneficial to me. Like this is a small group and the other people were nice and friendly. I mean, it wasn't that I had any issues with anybody, but their take on these support things was just like a social outing, like, "Well, today we have this meeting and we just all get together and talk about what we've been doing recently and what we're going to do." And it's like, "I don't need that." I get that from my family and my neighbors, you know?
>
> —Spouse caregiver of Vietnam veteran, unspecified service

Several caregivers discussed relying on, and sometimes preferring, informal support from their personal networks, including family and friends.

> Yes, I think there is nothing like professional in that capacity, but obviously friends and family are a great support system for venting and if we need help, and that kind of stuff, they're always willing to—they may not be local, but they're always willing to help.
>
> —Brother-in-law caregiver of post-9/11-era Navy veteran

For some caregivers, their religious community provided an important source of support:

> I am a believer, I go to church, and I surround myself with my church members who were very supportive . . . again, just support in anything I needed. If I needed to go someplace, they were willing to take me. Just those types of things.
>
> —Family member caregiver of Vietnam Navy veteran

And finally, some caregivers discussed being excluded from available supports. One caregiver mentioned that they were turned down from a caregiver support group that was tailored to a specific diagnosis, making it difficult to find an escape:

> Like last year I was really, really getting affected by this and I was trying to get caretaker—like, there's caretaker support groups. And I was denied from joining caretaker support groups because they would only accept people who were caretaking for people with dementia. And I'm like, "Okay, he's bedridden. It's a full-time job, like, he has cognitive issues, but it's not like full blown dementia." And they're like, "Sorry, he, again, he's not sick enough for us to extend you, or to invite you into the group so you can get support for your caretaking stress."
>
> —Partner caregiver of post-9/11-era Navy veteran

Another discussed being turned down from "support" available from VA, although the nature of this support was not specified:

> I mean, I could get support probably through the VA if I pushed it, but I'm not doing that. I mean, they already turned me down once. So I don't understand why—I mean, I'm here enough. I care for him at least 50 percent of the time. . . . I said I'm a very close family friend and I said [we're] not married, not that relationship. And they said, "Well, because you're the family, close friend, or whatever, we don't give to them, we would prefer to have outside sources come in because sometimes family is just too close to the situation." So which I think is silly because family sometimes knows the best way to handle things or friends, close friends.
>
> —Friend caregiver of post-9/11-era Navy veteran

CHAPTER 5

Caregiver Identities, Portrayals, and Interactions

The RAND team designed recruitment for these interviews as a mechanism to shed light on the needs and well-being of the most hidden of hidden heroes, due to the limited evidence base exploring their experiences. Caregivers were selected for interviews to reflect a range of diverse experiences with regard to gender, sexual orientation, race and ethnicity, relationship to the care recipient, and care recipients' health-related conditions. (Appendix A provides additional detail on the methodological approach and composition of the interviewee sample.)

Emerging from the Shadows takes a new approach to identifying caregivers by not relying on caregivers to identify as such. Instead, the survey asks whether individuals perform at least one of a series of tasks that would constitute caregiving (Ramchand et al., 2024). By using this approach, many more individuals were identified as caregivers than in previous research, including those who may not identify as such. Thus, interviewers asked how interviewees felt about being a caregiver and pursued additional lines of inquiry designed to explore whether or how these characteristics might impact their experiences as caregivers.

Caregivers Felt Both Similar to and Different from Other Caregivers

Interviewers inquired whether and why caregivers felt similar to or different from other caregivers. In some ways, caregivers felt similar to other caregivers in that they shared experiences common to the caregiving role.

> No. I mean, talking to people, they all have the same problems. The people they take care of are argumentative and they don't remember stuff.
>
> —Friend caregiver of Vietnam Army veteran

> No, it's the same. I have several friends who are caregivers as well. And some of their husbands have the same conditions, some have different conditions, but the reality for us is exactly the same.
>
> —Spouse caregiver of post-9/11-era Army veteran

> No. I don't think I'm any more unique than anyone else who does it. You love someone. Again, it's hard enough taking care of yourself. So taking care of someone—and quite frankly it depends on the person's disposition. It's obviously much more difficult if a person has dementia, Alzheimer's, something like that where anything could happen. They may be okay one minute and not okay the next, that's a different dynamic. But in [the care recipient's] case, we knew he knew what was going to happen and we did what we had to do. I don't think I'm any different than anybody else.
>
> —Family member caregiver of Vietnam Navy veteran

However, caregivers were also mixed on feeling similar to or different from other caregivers, often citing similar reasons for why their experiences might be easier or more difficult than those of others. As described later in this chapter, overall, caregivers were more likely to mention differences that were due to "achieved" characteristics (e.g., work, socioeconomic, or care recipient health-related conditions and needs) rather than differences that were due to "ascribed" characteristics (e.g., gender, race and ethnicity, sexual orientation).

Caregivers Recognized the Impact of Socioeconomic Status

Military and veteran caregivers come from various socioeconomic backgrounds: Between 16 and 21 percent have household incomes over $100,000, and one-third have incomes below 130 percent of the federal poverty limit (Ramchand et al., 2024). Caregivers highlighted differences in their socioeconomic statuses and those of other caregivers, discussing the added benefits afforded through having financial resources.

> Potentially, I think we have the means to do a lot of these things. And I think that's probably why we're able to adjust and be flexible and step up and do that. Whereas I think that might not be the case across the board, which could make it more challenging for others.
>
> —Son-in-law caregiver of Army veteran

> I would mostly say background. We're not really wealthy. So, I think that'll play a big part. Like if you have money, it seems like you can do a lot. Most of the doctors and the VA, all the good services, is like for the less wealthy people. We just get, like, they're not in a hurry or you get not-so-good services.
>
> —Adult grandchild caregiver of Air Force veteran

Health Care Experience Helped Some Caregivers

In addition to socioeconomic status, which might position some caregivers to experience advantages in their role as caregivers, some caregivers highlighted their medical or health care backgrounds as uniquely providing helpful knowledge and understanding as they fulfilled their caregiving responsibilities. One caregiver who expressed feeling similar to other caregivers also perceived their familiarity with the medical community to be an asset.

> My education . . . and I've worked in nursing homes. I have [a] physical therapy background. I raised an autistic son. So I know that I have the patience and a little bit of the understanding of people who are disabled and stuff. So in that sense, I feel like I do [have a different experience]. I also have a background in massage therapy and reflexology, that thing. So I think that helps with his exercises or if he says he's got pains in his legs or whatever, just to give him that massage, that rub down, that helps that nerve settle down.
>
> —Friend caregiver of post-9/11–era Navy veteran

> I've had a career in health care. So, I kind of know how things work. I know the system, I don't get frustrated with waits, and sometimes the waits are longer than you want, but I understand where it comes from.
>
> —Spouse caregiver of Vietnam veteran, unspecified service

Care Recipient Health-Related Conditions and Related Needs Affected Perceptions of Shared Experiences

As described in Chapter 3, caregivers' duties are as varied as the conditions the individuals they are caring for may have. The nature of care recipients' health-related conditions and resulting needs influenced whether caregivers felt that their experiences were similar to or different from those of other caregivers. Among those believing their experiences were different, caregivers shared the following:

> I mean, the one thing to remember when you're dealing with someone with dementia is that, as someone said to me during an Alzheimer's Association meeting I was at, when you've met one person with dementia, you've met one person with dementia. . . . I currently live in a retirement community, and so I have support from other people who have gone through this or who are going through this. And quite frequently, their situation was such that their spouse was gone very quickly. My husband's progression has been very, very slow. . . . So I can tell you that my experience has been the same as everyone else, but my experience has been different from everybody else. And anyone who's a caregiver will tell you the same thing. We all have the same experiences, but we all have very different experiences. We all have different abilities.
>
> —Spouse caregiver of Vietnam Air Force veteran

> I also think what makes it unique, too, is just that he is so independent. . . . I feel like, more on the physical side of things, I don't have to help him get dressed. I don't have to help him get cleaned up; like, he's done. It's not that. I think compared to some others who do this type of stuff, I think I actually have it a lot easier.
>
> —Nephew caregiver of Cold War–era Navy veteran

Notably, one caregiver described feeling that the medical community differentiated between supports provided to caregivers and care recipients based on the nature of care recipients' health-related conditions:

> The only thing that I could think of is his diagnosis. I think it, depending on the diagnosis, organizations or medical communities are more willing to offer help based off of the diagnosis of the person being taken care of, which sucks. . . . The VA, the health, all of them. . . . But the view on it is like, "Well, you could live a totally normal life," and it's like not for a severe migraine sufferer, if someone's like, "Oh, I have a migraine once a month or once every six months." "Sure." But when you have them daily or on a continuous basis, and then you have a rare form of migraine that has no cure, no treatment, no nothing. And exacerbated by all these mental health conditions on top of it, like that really makes it more difficult, and it's just a lot about perception of sort of these unseen medical conditions or ones that aren't seen as so severe. Like it's awful to say this, but if [the care recipient] had cancer that would be a lot different, like, totally different sort of approach because I said, "Oh, he has cancer," versus if I say, "Well, he has chronic severe migraines."
>
> —Partner caregiver of post-9/11-era Navy veteran

Caregivers Often Report Varying Degrees of Representation in Media Portrayals of Caregivers

When asked whether they felt represented by stories and other portrayals of military and veteran caregivers they saw or heard, caregivers were mixed in their perceptions. Some caregivers told the interviewers that they had not seen military and veteran caregivers in the media:

> To be quite honest with you. I don't hear a lot of stories unless you're speaking to something specifically. But I don't come across too many stories from a military perspective.
>
> —Son-in-law caregiver of Army veteran

> To be perfectly honest, I really haven't seen a lot of stories about caregivers. So, I guess, I don't know, but I never felt like, "Oh God, there's nobody out there that will help me."
>
> —Sibling caregiver of Army veteran

However, many felt represented through stories of caregivers, describing that even given their unique contexts, there are shared experiences and goals for caretaking among military and veteran caregivers.

> Yes. All the good that they [caregivers] say they provide or that they do to help with everyday life.
>
> —Friend caregiver of World War II Army veteran

> I think every caregiver's story is different, depending on the case. But I think they all share a similarity, which is trying to care for the person correctly.
>
> —Friend caregiver of veteran, unspecified service

That said, some caregivers did suggest differences in how the media portrayed caregivers relative to their own experiences. They believed that the media portrayed those who "had it harder," had different approaches to caregivers, or were different because of ascribed characteristics, specifically gender identity and race and ethnicity. Others described "kernels of truth" that represented parts of their experiences but not the entirety.

Some Caregivers Believe Others Have It Harder

Some caregivers did not feel represented by stories of caregivers because they felt that such stories demonstrated that their roles were easier than those of others:

> I haven't seen anything like that recently. I think I probably had an easier time than people who were much older or didn't have a very good health insurance plan.
>
> —Spouse caregiver of Vietnam veteran, unspecified service

> Well, one thing, and I do feel blessed that—I have absolutely no idea how caregivers do it if they have to tend to little children at the same time or have a full-time job or two full-time jobs or two jobs and have to do this full time. It would be absolutely exhausting. . . . That's probably the thing that always strikes me the most when I read about other caregivers is they have all of these other constraints, and financial [constraints].
>
> —Adult child caregiver of Navy Reserves veteran

Others Believe Themselves to Be More Caring

A few caregivers also felt that their own approaches were more caring and appropriate than those portrayed in stories of caregivers, and they felt that their relationships were different from those portrayed.

> I mean, I hear bad things about care providers, but, no, I don't think about that, because I'm not that type of person, you know? I make sure my dad's well taken care of, and if there's any issues, I'm on it, because I'm not going to let my dad be mistreated or anything. . . . I don't hear of very many daughters taking care of their fathers, I don't.
>
> —Adult child caregiver of Vietnam Navy veteran

> I've seen some things in the news about some caregivers, and I just feel that not everybody, it's like some nurses, not everybody is there for—to have the compassion. Some of them just do it for the money, which is okay. But it's like, you really have to like what you're doing. I never [expected] really to do this and it kind of like, fell on my lap. . . . I was still working. I had to quit my job.
>
> —Adult child caregiver of Korean War veteran, unspecified service

In their response, one caregiver described how such stories can often highlight caregiver infractions rather than positive examples:

> Absolutely not because, you know, speaking of that group, the lady had posted a video not too long ago of an elderly woman with dementia in a nursing home and the caregiver like physically abusing her... . . . And so [that] kind of gives in-home caregivers a bad rep when those kind of things are brought to light, not the ones who volunteer their time for people, you know?
>
> —Neighbor caregiver of Army veteran

In contrast, another caregiver emphasized that advertised stories of military and veteran caregivers were incomplete, potentially overemphasizing the positive aspects of caregiving:

> And the way that they talk about them, it's a false statement. . . . They're explaining it the way you want to hear it, not the way that it actually is. That's how I feel. I mean, it's not an honest story, reading it, you can just feel, that's not right. They're just doing what people want to hear, they're saying what people want to hear and not the negative. There's a lot of positive, but there's also negative.
>
> —Friend caregiver of post-9/11-era Navy veteran

Few Caregivers Mentioned Ascribed Characteristics

A couple of caregivers highlighted similarities in their gender and racial and ethnic identities with those of military and veteran caregivers represented in stories, but their comments suggest that other caregivers may feel alienated. For example, one caregiver reported:

> A lot of times when I hear about caregivers, I always feel like it's a woman usually. I feel kind of represented in that aspect.
>
> —Neighbor caregiver of veteran, unspecified service

Yet, survey research indicates that between 42 and 47 percent of military and veteran caregivers are men (Ramchand et al., 2024).

Another caregiver found alliance among their group of Latino caregivers:

> Well, a lot of times yes, because it all depends also on what it is that's going on. For example, if it's a topic related to mental life, well, you feel very identified. . . . [W]e are a very large group of Latinos who are affected in everything, carrying our husbands, it's a very large group.
>
> —Spouse caregiver of post-9/11-era Army veteran

Caregivers Developed Strategies to Garner Respect from Health Care Teams, but Some Reported Negative Interactions

Caregivers were asked whether they felt respected and understood by health care professionals, which, as described in Chapter 3, may affect their experience navigating health care systems. In *Emerging from the Shadows*, only one-third of military and veteran caregivers felt that providers always listened to them (Ramchand et al., 2024). In contrast, in these interviews, many caregivers believed that their voices were heard. However, those who felt heard discussed certain strategies (e.g., patient advocacy, a familiarity with medical terminology) that helped garner this respect. Others recounted instances of negative interactions and a negative perception of the U.S. health care system in general.

Many Caregivers Had Positive Experiences with Health Care Teams

Many caregivers emphasized that health care professionals took time to listen to them and explain diagnoses, treatments, and other health care decisions.

> Yeah, we've had to, in all of his medical appointments I've gone to him with, I have to help talk with him because he can't hear or understand most of the people he's talking with. So, they've been very respectful and understanding about needing to speak up or speak to me, and I can raise my voice a little bit to him so he can understand better.
>
> —Adult child caregiver of Navy Reserves veteran

> Definitely I think I get treated really well when we go into the doctor's office and whatnot, when they're sitting there talking to me. I don't know, maybe it's because it's family, and I'm willing to put up my time for it and not go the extra route of finding a caregiver to provide that service. I think I get treated really well. . . . I think the way I'm being spoken to. The appreciation of me taking out my time out of my life to do services like this for my own family and not putting it on an outside source or service.
>
> —Son-in-law/nephew caregiver of veterans, unspecified services

Some Caregivers Deployed Purposeful Strategies to Improve Provider Relationships

Caregivers who felt listened to by health care teams elaborated on strategies they used to garner such respect. One strategy was patient advocacy. One caregiver stressed the importance of caregiver advocacy:

> I mean, again, to be a real advocate I can be real pushy in a way. In order to get what he needs, you know? I think that's . . . helped us survive a lot.
>
> —Partner caregiver of post-9/11-era Navy veteran

Another caregiver similarly shared:

> Yes, everyone's been really amazing. . . . I mean, just like calling as, you know, "I'm not a guardian, I'm not him." So, it can be confusing when you're talking to someone who hasn't necessarily dealt with a caregiver before, but you explain your situation and people are—I feel like they try to help more when you tell them who you are and what you're trying to achieve. So, yes.
>
> —Brother-in-law caregiver of post-9/11-era Navy veteran

Another strategy these caregivers mentioned was being able to speak to health care providers in "terminology" that providers understood, often afforded by having a background in health care:

> I do now. It took a long time for them to just want to have more open discussions about his disabilities and stuff because they just look at you like you're stupid or something. And when I started using their terminology, that was respected—I had to do a little bit of reading and research—and then it's like I taught myself. "Let's try it this way, let's use their terminology." And when I did, then I got the respect from them where they would talk to me. And if I didn't understand it, I would also say, "Would you please make it simpler for me to understand because you used a few terms I'm not familiar with?" And then they would do that, too, out of respect for you because they know that you're, I guess worthy—maybe that's the word.
>
> —Friend caregiver of post-9/11-era Navy veteran

> I believe so, yeah. I just think their approach and my approach in a situation that I have a background and caregiving. I feel like because I have been doing that and have done it before, I know how to interact and communicate with those other professionals.
>
> —Neighbor caregiver of veteran, unspecified service

Some Offered Examples of Negative Interactions

Among those who did not feel respected and understood by health care professionals, the common drivers were experiences of poor "quality" or challenges with interpersonal communication.

> No. Because a couple of months ago, my dad's doctor and nurse practitioner told my dad that I was using him and that he didn't need me. And that right there really did it because I don't use my dad. I work, I take care of my dad. It's my responsibility. They don't know, you know what I'm saying? They don't know our everyday living. I wish people would understand what I do for my dad and what type of responsibility it is, but some people don't know and don't see what I have to do and how much stress it puts on me sometimes.
>
> —Adult child caregiver of Vietnam Navy veteran

> Do I feel respected by the VA lady? No. I guess maybe because I chose to help a man that I started caring about and who had nobody. And I don't, like—I guess I don't, like, have formal training, and because I choose to volunteer my time for the man, I feel like she doesn't treat me as like an equal caregiver, if you will.
>
> —Neighbor caregiver of Army veteran

Notably, among caregivers who felt respected and understood by health care professionals, a few also mentioned prior negative interactions. One caregiver shared that when this occurs, they typically switch doctors:

> There are some that I feel like, "Hello, I'm over here. Listen to me now. I've been doing this a long time. I understand what's going on." And that doesn't happen very often because I usually don't see those physicians again. But the primaries that I've ever dealt with, the neuroscientists, the neurologists, the geri psych [geriatric psychiatrist], I felt comfortable with them that they trusted my ability to care for my husband.
>
> —Spouse caregiver of Vietnam Air Force veteran

Another caregiver described their unique difficulties finding a reliable home health aide:

> It was very hard to get someone to come to his house. The lady that we had, I need to probably tell you, that the lady that we had, she was a really good caregiver, and she did a wonderful job, but we found out that she was stealing money from his charge cards.
>
> —Partner caregiver of Korean War–era Navy veteran

A Few Shared Negative Perceptions of Health Care Overall

Finally, a few caregivers, including those who did and did not feel respected and understood by health care professionals, described concerns with health care systems generally.

> I feel like they're going to try to give you results, but at the end it's about money, everything's about money. So, they want to say if they gave a resolution even though it wasn't the right one.
>
> —Adult grandchild caregiver of Air Force veteran

> I don't really talk to them as much as [the care recipient] does. I just accompany him. But I honestly think these people are just so burnt out. I think they're so overwhelmed, and I think that these veterans are just a number. . . . And I think that's come with a whole different set of problems. The PTSD, they have their own set of issues, and it really takes a kind, compassionate doctor. And I think a lot of them are just desensitized and just running through.
>
> —Spouse caregiver of post-9/11-era Army veteran

> Well, I mean, that's in general, I think even dealing with your own health, doctors are always going to treat everybody who isn't a doctor as inferior, but the nurses and practitioners and assistants and so forth are usually much more responsive. I think that's just the way that health care system is set up. I don't think that has anything to do with home health caregivers.
>
> —Adult child caregiver of Korean War Army veteran

Caregiver Experiences Were Grounded Within Achieved Characteristics Instead of Ascribed Characteristics

Appendix A lists the military and veteran caregiver subgroups specifically emphasized in recruitment efforts, given their underrepresentation in caregiver research. These subgroups were largely oriented around ascribed characteristics, such as caregivers who identify as male, as LGBTQ+, and/or as part of racial and ethnic minority groups (in addition to those sampled in relation to the care recipient and care recipient condition). However, the analyses presented in this chapter demonstrate that when caregivers were asked about differences in their experiences, whether positive or negative, they almost always attributed those differences as stemming from achieved characteristics rather than ascribed ones. These achieved characteristics included experience within the health care sector (as described previously) and socioeconomic status, as well as relational and citizenship status.

For instance, across the interviews, a few caregivers spoke to the differences in their relationships with care recipients compared with what they believed to be stereotypical. In response to whether they believed they were similar to or different from other caregivers, one caregiver stated,

> Yes and no. No, I don't want to say it makes it different, because I try my best, because I was a stay-at-home mom to try to keep him at home as long as we could without putting him somewhere . . . but I think because I primarily took it on that it was a bit difficult,

> because most of the time it's the children, their children that take it on and not the grandchildren. In that part I would say, yes.
>
> —Adult grandchild caregiver of Army veteran

In addition, another caregiver stated that although they felt somewhat represented in caregiver stories, their being a permanent resident in the United States set them apart from citizens:

> So, I definitely feel like I'm represented, but probably like you said, not exactly, because, because of that, you know, being a permanent resident means I can't represent myself in terms of voting and that kind of stuff. So, I can feel left out in the political landscape that other caregivers, you know, have a say that they vote for which in effect, you know, the stipends or the VA, or whatever.
>
> —Brother-in-law caregiver of post-9/11-era Navy veteran

Notably, the sole exceptions who referenced ascribed characteristics were the two caregivers discussed within this chapter who respectively referenced their gender identity and ethnicity as driving their perceptions of feeling represented in caregiver stories.

CHAPTER 6

Economic Impacts of Caregiving

Emerging from the Shadows presents an in-depth examination of the economic and financial toll of caregiving. Some key findings from that report in this regard include the following:

- Military and veteran caregivers incur approximately $8,583 per year in out-of-pocket costs associated with caregiving.
- Military and veteran caregivers forgo approximately $4,522 in household income per year.
- Just over half of military and veteran caregivers have set aside emergency or rainy-day funds that would cover their expenses for three months, in case of sickness, job loss, economic downturn, or other emergencies (Ramchand et al., 2024).

These findings prompted the RAND team to ask caregivers a series of questions about whether and how they were planning for the future; whether they were worried about their own age or their care recipients' advancing age and whether that would affect their physical or financial ability to continue providing care; whether caregiving responsibilities had affected their work or education, finances, and income; and what, if any, out-of-pocket expenses they incurred as a result of their caregiving responsibilities. Caregiver responses to these questions varied substantially; there were significant differences between those who had adequate resources to meet needs now and in the future and those who did not, as well as between those who were already retired and those who were still working.

Many Caregivers Are Not Comprehensively Planning for the Future

Several of those interviewed were not planning for the future or worried about potential changing circumstances at all but instead live in the moment.

> Well, hopefully he doesn't get any worse. I'm not planning for the future right now.
>
> —Friend caregiver of Vietnam Army veteran

> Right now, there's no real plan. Yeah. I take it one day at a time.
>
> —Adult child caregiver of Cold War–era Navy veteran

In addition, two caregivers shared hope (but not concrete plans) that the care recipient would require less care in the future.

> I hope things get better with the [currently broken] hips so he can start doing this stuff on his own.
>
> —Partner caregiver of Army veteran

> Well, I am actually optimistic now because they are going to send him to the—they're finally getting these appointments in order for him. I'm really, really hoping that once we get all these levels evened out, that he's going to show a vast improvement.
>
> —Spouse caregiver of post-9/11-era Army veteran

Several caregivers expressed only near-term plans for the care recipient, such as one caregiver who expressed a desire to get their older adult care recipient grandfather outside more often. Another caregiver expressed plans for the care recipient, a friend, "to continue her physical therapies, her occupational therapies." A third caregiver said:

> To get him stronger, to get him healthier so he can do more on his own. Because when he does do things on his own, he is very proud of that. It makes him feel good. A sense of pride, a sense of accomplishment, and that is a big goal that I have is I want him to feel like he can accomplish things.
>
> —Friend caregiver of post-9/11-era Navy veteran

Some caregivers are also pondering the future in a somewhat general way. For example, some caregivers anticipated that they would need to transition into a smaller or more accessible home at some point and were considering whether assisted living would be necessary in the future. However, they were not very advanced in this type of planning:

> Right now, our plan is to stay in this house, because we just moved here, for a period of ten years. And then at that point, we'll have to take a look at the situation. Decide if we're going to move into an apartment or what in some senior facility at that point. There's always a possibility it might have to happen sooner, but we will deal with it at that point.
>
> —Spouse caregiver of Vietnam Army veteran

> I mean, as [the care recipient] gets older and he gets weaker, his immobility is really going to be bad and his other arm, I fear he's going to have a stroke again and all these things, and I do not know with the future. I hope that at that time, the VA lady really

> kicks in and figures out something. So that's if not—I mean, full time at my house has been thrown out there.
>
> —Neighbor caregiver of Army veteran

Finally, some caregivers related having fairly detailed plans in place:

> Right now, we're trying to move. We live in a single-family dwelling and it's an old house that requires a lot of work and the yard, and we're not able to do that anymore. So, we're looking at moving into a condo that would be on the ground floor and would demand less time and energy from us . . . we have wills, we have durable power of attorney. We have long-term care, which, we've had that for almost 20 years now, I think.
>
> —Spouse caregiver of Vietnam veteran, unspecified service

> As far as what the future holds for the two of us, I think everything is in place for what we need to have and what we need to do. I've got all of my documents in place for myself and for him. I've got my kids on everything that I have. . . . I've moved into a retirement community so that I know that there's someone here to take care of issues if I'm unable to handle them. I'm a bit of a planner.
>
> —Spouse caregiver of Vietnam Air Force veteran

Caregivers Differed in Their Abilities to Cover Out-of-Pocket Costs

As potentially indicated by the wide range of socioeconomic backgrounds of caregivers previously described in Chapter 5, caregivers differed greatly in their abilities to cover out-of-pocket costs. For instance, some caregivers were acutely aware of high costs related to caregiving but were able to absorb them:

> I just calculated the taxes, what our medical expenses are. And I think that in 2023 it was $25,000, just the medical costs for him.
>
> —Partner caregiver of post-9/11-era Navy veteran

> Several years ago, he was able to get long-term care insurance. So, that was able to assist us with that. When he went into care, I started working with the elder law attorney that I have to get him qualified for Medicaid, because [state] is a very good state, and it allows the wife to take the assets. There's a lot of complications to go through that, a lot of hoops you have to jump, but it does get him qualified for Medicaid. So, even though the cost of his care is $14,000 a month, about $5,000 of that is paid by his long-term care insurance. There is a small supplement that the VA provides. I still have to pay $3,000 a month. . . . Prior to him going into care, we had his Social Security, my Social Security, and my retire-

ment. Now I have to live on my Social Security and my retirement. All of his Social Security goes to pay for his care.

—Spouse caregiver of Vietnam Air Force veteran

Other caregivers referenced increased costs but indicated that they were minimal or easily absorbed:

I would say I really don't. I mean, we drive to his doctor's appointments and therapy sessions and things, but that's minor. I mean, in comparison to paying medical bills.

—Spouse caregiver of Vietnam veteran, unspecified service

Food, health and beauty things, household things, like, for instance, cleaning supplies, toilet paper, paper towels, food for both of us, you know? And if we got to go somewhere, gas money, finding transportation or anything that may pop up that we need. 200, maybe 300 a month.

—Adult child caregiver of Vietnam Navy veteran

In other cases, the care recipient was able to cover any needed expenses from their own budget or benefits:

I have not paid out of pocket for that stuff. He's still able to pay for all of that. So those aren't expenses that I've had to incur personally.

—Adult child caregiver of Navy Reserves veteran

Sometimes I'll go to the grocery store first, like I'll go there on the way and a couple of, there's just a few necessities that he's gonna need without scanning his fridge, and I'll pick those up on the way over there and drop them off. I'm having a day where I don't have a bunch of time, but he always reimburses me. . . . He's very, very, financially independent, I guess you can say.

—Nephew caregiver of Cold War–era Navy veteran

However, in some cases, caregivers broadly expressed concern about the costs:

Just things are—we've had a lot of expenses as far as like the ramps to get to the house, the wheelchairs. They break down after a while; you have to get new ones. Getting these exercise items so that he can build his strength in his arms, getting the car adjusted, and he's on his third car that we had to get the gears put on to do that. It's more expensive, it adds to the expenses in general. Just, it adds up.

—Partner caregiver of post-9/11-era Navy veteran

Toiletries specific for her, and then also again with the dementia, even though I get the SNAP [Supplemental Nutrition Assistance Program] benefits, she's very wasteful because

> her mind changes so quick, she says she wants something that she doesn't, and I have to make something else, so we've wasted a lot of food.
>
> —Adult grandchild caregiver of Air Force veteran

Caregiving Responsibilities Hit Those Who Have to Work Outside the Home Hardest

Many interviewees were retired, so the added responsibilities of caregiving did not affect their ability to work or their household incomes. For example, when asked whether caregiving affected her income or finances, the partner caregiver of a Korean War–era Navy veteran noted, "No, it did not. I'm fortunate that I have a nice retirement." Similarly, the spouse caregiver of a Vietnam veteran of an unspecified service said, "No, I'm retired. So, it didn't affect our income."

However, among those who do work, work accommodations were mentioned by two caregivers as helpful, particularly the ability to telework:

> [F]ortunately for me, being at home helped tremendously. Because I was able to watch him, still work, and do what I needed to do for him and the job. And I think that was the saving grace. If I was away from the home . . . of course, it would have been totally different.
>
> —Family member caregiver of Vietnam Navy veteran

> I mean, to do anything else, take care of yourself . . . cuts into work and everything else. I was working remotely, which is why I was here, but even then, I still have to be at my desk working, and I couldn't be in there.
>
> —Adult child caregiver of Korean War Army veteran

Unfortunately, less than half of working military and veteran caregivers are offered telework options. Possibly for this reason, 16 percent of military and veteran caregivers had cut back their work hours, and 11 percent switched jobs (Ramchand et al., 2024). During these interviews, some caregivers acknowledged that caregiving responsibilities had limited or changed their abilities to work:

> Well, I don't work very much anymore. This is a full-time job almost.
>
> —Friend caregiver of post-9/11-era Navy veteran

> Maybe just in the sense of my being tired. I feel like I don't, and sometimes I just think I can't keep working for long because I'm so wore out from taking care of others. . . . I don't think work has been impacted. I made adjustments to try and allow, like I work longer. Well, I guess that would impact because I changed to ten-hour days so that I would have

more time on Friday to be getting groceries and buying what [care recipient] needs, and for my own household. So, yeah, I guess that has impacted.

—Sibling caregiver of Cold War–era veteran, unspecified service

A few caregivers mentioned engaging in micro-entrepreneurial activities that allowed them to supplement their incomes in flexible ways that accommodated their caregiving responsibilities; however, one grandchild caregiver of an Air Force veteran noted that painting nails only provided "[pocket] change."

I'm also a dog groomer, I work from here from my home, so I can handle the economic situation. . . . [D]ue to the fact that I'm working from home, my income doesn't change. If I go to work outside the home, then they take me away from being a caregiver much faster, because I can't leave my husband alone. That's why I have the business at home.

—Spouse caregiver of post-9/11-era Army veteran

No, [my income is] half that much. I do physical therapy on the side, or I'll travel to somebody's home to do that, or I can do massages in my home. I have a room that I dedicate to that for people who want to make appointments and stuff.

—Friend caregiver of post-9/11-era Navy veteran

One interviewee seemed to indicate that she had stepped away from her role caring for her veteran neighbor because of the inability to balance work, education, and caregiving responsibilities. Another caregiver described the need for supplemental help from others to maintain her own employment:

When he was sick, yes, because I would have to leave him here and, I mean, I got my son that helps me, but he lives like 20 minutes away. And, yes, I work right down the road, but like that's my job too, but I just got a secondary job—I found out today. I'm just going to have to get a little bit more help hopefully from my sister or friends or something just in case something would happen and I'm at work and I can't get right there right away. Just somebody that can help me.

—Adult child caregiver of Vietnam Navy veteran

Accessibility of VA Support Was Meaningful, If It Was Accessible

Those who were able to access VA care or services often brought up how useful that support was, specifically crediting VA for keeping them from being worse off:

I'd have to say [caregiving] really hasn't [affected our finances] because so much of his care is provided for or paid for by the VA that we're not in a situation. I mean, I know

> that you read stories about people as they get older and one of the partners gets a chronic debilitating disease or cancer or something and people end up selling their home to pay medical bills. I don't believe that we'll ever be in that situation because of his care through the VA.
>
> —Spouse caregiver of Vietnam veteran, unspecified service

> So with the VA, thank God for those benefits, everything worked out. He did not have to come out of pocket for too much of anything. And so that really did not affect me and it didn't really affect him financially.
>
> —Family member caregiver of Vietnam Navy veteran

However, those unable to access VA support often expressed some degree of frustration:

> [M]y husband did not qualify for the VA benefits. What occurred was prior to about 1985/86, he had used the VA because it was convenient to where he was working. When we moved to a different location and our health care benefits became better, he no longer used the VA. So, when he was diagnosed in 2013, I immediately decided to sign him back up for VA benefits because I didn't know what they might provide for him. And that's when I was advised that because he hadn't used the VA since 2003 and because of our income level, he no longer qualified. Don't ask me how angry that makes me.
>
> —Spouse caregiver of Vietnam Air Force veteran

> Well, I mean, I know I've talked to a lot of gentlemen that get VA help. And I mean, a lot of them seem to be more financially better off than what we are. And so, that part I really don't understand how they can get it and we can't, you know what I'm saying? So, I mean even if [VA help] was with his medications, nothing else, that will help tremendously.
>
> —Spouse caregiver of Air Force veteran

Few specifically mentioned VA's Program of Comprehensive Assistance for Family Caregivers (PCAFC). Those who did expressed ambivalence and concern about the program. For instance, one expressed a belief that then-proposed VA cuts to the program were being made in ways designed to target her ethnic group, although this caregiver did not provide further reasons driving this belief.

> We applied for [the PCAFC stipend], and they were basically like, "He's not bad enough. You're not giving him a bath or wiping his butt. So, we're not going to give you any money." I was like, "Well, okay then." But I'm glad I don't have to do those things. I'd rather not do those things and get the money.
>
> —Spouse caregiver of post-9/11-era Army veteran

> VA pays me a monthly allowance. What happens is that now . . . they made a decision to eliminate all the caregivers of the people who were in the war from Iraq and Afghanistan.

If the person doesn't need a 100-percent caregiver to help them physically, they want to remove the caregiver. They forget that they sent totally, 100-percent healthy people, and they not only sent them back physically damaged, but mentally damaged. And there's a lot of mental damage, there's a lot of people taking their lives, a lot of veterans taking their lives because of this. And we caregivers are doing the work, and making sure that these veterans stay alive. . . . And now, wanting to take away our caregiver, it's precisely all the Latinas that they want us out.

—Spouse caregiver of post-9/11-era Army veteran

CHAPTER 7

Changes in Care Recipient–Caregiver Relationships

Caregivers' relationships to care recipients vary. Figure 7.1 presents data on the relationships between military and veteran caregivers and those they are caring for, separated between those caring for someone 60 years of age or under and those caring for someone over 60 years of age.

The diversity of these relationships warrants further investigation. Interviewed caregivers were asked to describe whether and how their relationship with care recipients had changed given their roles as caregivers and whether and how they found their caregiving responsibilities to be rewarding.

FIGURE 7.1
Military and Veteran Caregivers' Relationship to the Care Recipient

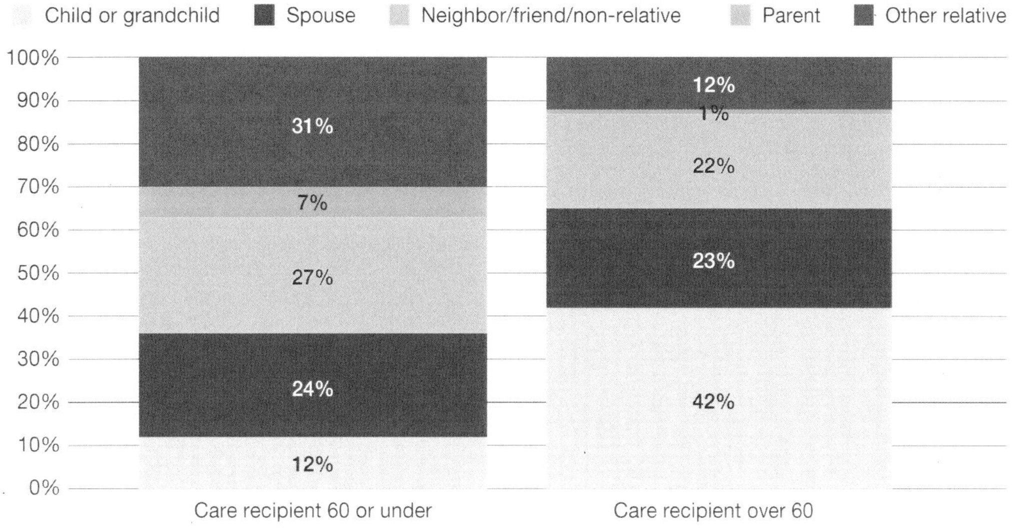

SOURCE: Data from Ramchand et al., 2024 (Table 1.3).

Most Care Recipient–Caregiver Relationships Changed

Overall, interviewees were mixed in their perspectives on whether their relationships with care recipients had changed and, if so, whether their relationships had experienced positive or challenging impacts.

Many Caregivers Described Positive Impacts

Many caregivers said that their relationships with care recipients had experienced positive impacts since the onset of their caregiving responsibilities. These caregivers emphasized feeling "closer" and more connected to care recipients through their caregiving relationship:

> It changed for the better. We didn't really have good communication. But when I started to come over more, there was a bond that we had, and I got to see him more. I got to talk to him about things that I don't really talk to my other family members about.
>
> —Adult grandchild caregiver of veteran, unspecified service

> It made us closer, actually. . . . We're more like family per se. It strengthened our friendship. It really did. So, it's made it like a little more personal: we watch movies together now and sometimes me being his caregiver—this is his words, not mine—he said sometimes that now that I'm his caregiver that I kind of take his mind off what's really happening, his pain and stuff like that.
>
> —Friend caregiver of Air Force veteran

Spouse caregivers stressed the notion of deepening their marriage commitment through their caregiver–care recipient relationship:

> I think he realizes how much he needs me to help him. And I think a lot of things, he don't know what he would do if he didn't have me.
>
> —Spouse caregiver of Air Force veteran

> Sometimes as a caregiver, you just feel like, what next? You feel like you can't get your head above water because if it's not this issue, and then we get this issue straightened out, then it's another issue. And it really, it makes you adhere to those marriage vows. It's easy to be married when things are great.
>
> —Spouse caregiver of post-9/11-era Army veteran

Some Described Relationships Experiencing Challenges over Time

Some caregivers expressed that their relationship with care recipients had experienced challenges over time; a few of them highlighted difficulties specifically stemming from the progression of care recipients' dementia:

> We are closer, but it is causing stress because the dementia is the worst. The violent outburst that comes with the disease or the dementia or forgetting who I am so she's not comfortable with me touching her.
>
> —Adult grandchild caregiver of Air Force veteran

> Well, being my dad, I was always close to my dad. But I would do anything that he needed. His grocery shopping, his finances, it all fell on me after that. And in the beginning when my dad was still, as I remembered him throughout the years, it was quite easy. Even though he was deaf, he could read my lips and we could still converse. But as he got older and probably within four or five months before he actually passed away, it became very difficult. Very difficult in that I don't—he was not diagnosed with dementia or Alzheimer's. But there was a point where he said, "And who are you?" And that's a very difficult thing for even now. I'm sorry, it's a very difficult thing when your parent looks at you and says, "Who are you?" And so, it changed our relationship a little bit because it was just very challenging to be in that position, yet still have to be there for him 24 hours a day.
>
> —Adult child caregiver of World War II Merchant Marine veteran

In addition, two caregivers described a difficult transition in their primary role, from partner to caretaker, and the ensuing loss of marital social and emotional support.

> I no longer have a companion. I no longer have a husband. As I was saying to someone else the other day whose husband is in care, we're not wives and we're not widows. And even though they are in care, we're still caregivers in many, many different ways. I guess the best thing to say is I have no companion and I have no one who is there for me, even though he would really want to be there for me.
>
> —Spouse caregiver of Vietnam Air Force veteran

> I don't feel like his partner, I feel like a nurse. And I experience burnout, a lot [of] frustration. I have a hard time, the times when he is well, like he wants to do stuff and everything, and I'm always really cautious because we never know when the symptoms might kick off. So I'm always watching out and trying to keep him from doing too much or eating the wrong things or whatever. So I don't feel like I'm in a relationship. I feel like I'm always taking care of someone and always have to be on duty.
>
> —Partner caregiver of post-9/11-era Navy veteran

Several Caregivers Said That There Was No Relationship Change

However, several caregivers did not believe that there had been any overall change to their relationships with care recipients.

> No, I mean, he's still my father. I think you just do what needs to be done.
>
> —Adult child caregiver of Cold War–era Army veteran

> Well, it just, it made me aware of our ages and made me kind of think about what's ahead because I may have to help him more in the future. But then he may have to help me in the future, too. So, it didn't really change our relationship. It changed my awareness of what's going on.
>
> —Spouse caregiver of Vietnam veteran, unspecified service

A Few Mentioned That They Initially Had Difficulty Adjusting

Finally, a few caregivers, both those who did and did not say that their relationship had changed, also noted the difficulties of initially adjusting to the newfound relationship of caregiver–care recipient.

> So [for] father-in-law, it was a lot of stress issues at the beginning, due to the typical relationship. I think now with the day-to-day, it's got a lot better with trust, and being able to listen has made a huge difference. With my uncle, there really hasn't been any issues there. It's just, I guess now being the one that's being relied on, I guess he has no choice but to be.
>
> —Son-in-law/nephew caregiver of veterans, unspecified services

> It made me look at him more in the person sense and not a grandfather's sense. It really just changed the whole dynamic because you see this mighty little guy who has never had fear, who still believes he can conquer anything that he does. To see him lose a little bit of spark again just makes me look at him, just more from a person's standpoint and not, "This is a grandfather," because now I just look at him like I can't just imagine like people who have it harder or what people have to do 24/7.
>
> —Adult grandchild caregiver of Army veteran

Most Caregivers Found Elements of Caregiving Rewarding

Emerging from the Shadows provides evidence that military and veteran caregivers report some personal gain from caregiving, including becoming aware of one's inner strengths, gaining self-confidence, growing as a person, and learning to do things they had not done before (Ramchand et al., 2024). Given that so much caregiving research is focused on the negative consequences of caregiving, these interviews sought to explore how caregivers benefit. When asked whether caregivers found their roles to be rewarding, almost all agreed. Reasons included knowing that the recipient is well cared for, enhanced relationships with the care recipient, and intrinsic rewards.

Knowing That the Recipient Is Well Cared for Is Meaningful for Many Caregivers

Many caregivers found ensuring that care recipients are taken care of to be the most rewarding aspect of caregiving.

> I think the biggest thing is just making sure she's cared for by people who love her. Emotionally—a sense of peace that you're not worried about her or where she is or how she's doing. . . . And then also, seeing her be happy. I think she's better being given care by her loved ones as opposed to people who are not that close to her . . . she always expresses how thankful she is and how much she loves us and appreciates us, helping her and taking care of her. So, as far as I'm concerned that makes it all worthwhile.
>
> —Son-in-law caregiver of Army veteran

> The most rewarding aspect is that I know that he's taken care of. Nobody can love him and take care of him as good as I can. And that's just part of the marriage. That's my duty as a spouse. I know that if the tables were turned, he would do the exact same for me.
>
> —Spouse caregiver of post-9/11-era Army veteran

In their responses, a few specifically shared their desire to ensure that care recipients could be kept out of nursing homes:

> I mean, the main reason we kept them at home, both [my sibling] and I had—when I was much, much younger, I worked in nursing homes and hospitals, and she had also had that experience, and neither of us would put a dog in either of those places. So that was the main reason. It wasn't a positive motivator. It was a negative motivator, I guess. . . . I mean, I think it's a very worthwhile thing to do if you can swing it when the opportunity presents itself in someone's life.
>
> —Adult child caregiver of Korean War Army veteran

> That even though in the end, like, she doesn't understand what's going on, when she does pass over, she was comfortable. I know that she's getting the right treatment. I didn't stick her in a nursing home or anything. I know she's getting treated fairly.
>
> —Adult grandchild caregiver of Air Force veteran

Some Reported Enjoying Enhanced Relationships

Several caregivers also shared that what they found rewarding was enjoying the time they spent with care recipients and feeling closer to or more connected with the care recipient.

> I love listening to his stories and he's been a lot of—he has been to a lot of places and seen a lot of things and I'm just very proud to be taking care of him. It's just putting a smile on their face, helping them do something that they didn't think they could do. We go for

> walks quite often. Just little short walks, and we try to go a couple of blocks at a time but sometimes we can't go that far. Because sometimes I'll [say], "Come on, we can do it," and he just doesn't think he can. But then when he does, it's just amazing.
>
> —Friend caregiver of World War II Army veteran

> I think the relationship we built has been super rewarding, but not only that like seeing him change and get better, we don't think he's ever going to be cured. I don't think he thinks he will be either but, you know, taking steps in the right direction and seeing improvement in areas we thought would never be improved, [can] just be really rewarding. But knowing that like it's bringing my family life and so closer to, closer to me and our family. So, it's really rewarding to have an uncle around and that kind of stuff as well. See my son grow and interact with [the care recipient] and those sorts of things.
>
> —Brother-in-law caregiver of post-9/11-era Navy veteran

Some Caregivers Experienced Intrinsic Rewards

Caregivers also highlighted personal reasons for finding their responsibilities to be rewarding. Several caregivers noted fulfilling their desire to help as being key:

> I think I'm one of those who is a natural caregiver, and so it does make you feel—it makes me feel very good to be helping someone else, especially a parent. I hope I'm setting an example of my kids when in 25 years they might have to do the same for me. But that it is rewarding to help others. We've lost that in our society of kind of that selflessness. But it is a very rewarding experience, again, as long as you don't burn yourself out, because I think it can also be a very draining thing.
>
> —Adult child caregiver of Navy Reserves veteran

> I like being able to help people. And whether it's my dad or somebody else, it makes me happy—to make them happy.
>
> —Adult child caregiver of Cold War–era Navy veteran

A few caregivers raised that feeling appreciated for their efforts was rewarding:

> Appreciation, gratitude. You feel that you are doing humanitarian work. You learn from their personal experiences, from their life.
>
> —Friend caregiver of veteran, unspecified service

> Well, I guess he has shown me the appreciation he says. He's very, very good about that. I know a lot of men don't do that.
>
> —Spouse caregiver of Air Force veteran

Some Caregivers Said That They Did Not Find Caregiving Rewarding

Two caregivers responded that they did not find the experience rewarding. Rather, they expressed that they were fulfilling their caregiving responsibilities out of a sense of obligation to and love for the care recipients, demonstrating the breadth of experiences faced by military and veteran caregivers.

> No. I'm sorry, there's nothing rewarding about caring for him. He's very grateful. He's very loving. He's very appreciative. But I don't find any joy in what I provide. I mean, I don't do it unpleasantly, don't misunderstand me. I do it in a very loving and caring way. And I love my husband very much and I will care for him as long as I possibly can. But there is no joy in caring for someone. . . . This is a commitment to my husband that I love, and I know that he would treat me the same way, and I don't find that rewarding. It's part of my life, it's part of my commitment to him. I don't resent it. I resent everything that's taken place, but I don't resent having to care for him.
>
> —Spouse caregiver of Vietnam Air Force veteran

> I don't think there is such a thing. You do it because you love the person and at the end of the day, like, that's kind of it. There is no rewarding aspect to it. There's nothing in this that makes you feel like, "Oh, I'm such an amazing person," or "I feel incredible," or" I'm helping them," or anything like that. I feel like if someone is caregiving and they're dealing with a lot, you just go day by day, and you hope and pray that you find a treatment or you can get them stabilized to a point where they could be functional, and you will not have to caretake. . . . It's just, if I don't do it, and there's a huge sense of guilt. If I don't do it, then what's going to happen to them, because they can't do it on their own and no one, no place is going to take them. So, who's going to do it?
>
> —Partner caregiver of post-9/11-era Navy veteran

CHAPTER 8

How Organizations Could Improve

One of the primary goals of most research into military and veteran caregiving is to provide insights that can be used to improve programs, policies, and, ultimately, the lives and well-being of caregivers and care recipients. Accordingly, the RAND team asked caregivers specifically what organizations could do better. Many caregivers made recommendations of varying levels of specificity, particularly around outreach and training. However, quite a few caregivers expressed that there was nothing they could think of, indicating that the support they had received was adequate, that they had no needs, or that they were unaware of what type of services could possibly be helpful.

Caregivers Asked for Increased Awareness About and Outreach to Military and Veteran Caregivers

As noted earlier, several caregivers mentioned that they had never seen military and veteran caregivers represented in media or advertisements, that they lacked adequate information on available benefits, or that they had experienced communications issues. These themes carried forward into their thoughts on how organizations could improve; several mentioned a desire for more outreach to increase awareness of available resources.

> I'm not looking and I'm sure that they're there, but maybe if they shouted out a little bit more on social media or something, and people, maybe not so much to me but people have family members who are having a tougher time know that there is this group, or the support system would be helpful.
>
> —Nephew caregiver of Cold War–era Navy veteran

> I mean, if this information honestly was available at your doctor's office, basically I'm saying, okay, look if you need some help or you need to reach out to somebody. . . . I know there is a senior care center in [name] County where I drop him off and he does things with other seniors, but something like that, I guess, would be helpful if it was more publicly available and advertised, where more people knew about this as a service that the county that you live in provides for the veterans or just seniors in general.
>
> —Adult child caregiver of Cold War–era Army veteran

Some Caregivers Sought Services to Address Specific Caregiving Needs

A few caregivers expressed needs for specific, concrete supportive services, such as assistance with household tasks, mental health services, or case management.

> The only thing that would help me if I had someone to help with house cleaning. I'm 75. Well, I will be 75 Sunday. . . . [J]ust knowing how to really deal with people with these medical conditions. And like it being diabetes, things to do that will stop him from only eating sweets. I think that would be the main thing.
>
> —Spouse caregiver of Air Force veteran

> If there's some type of assistance that we may need it [to] be there for me to go to and talk with somebody. Or if we need help with something or bills or something like that, somebody we can call and talk with, but there is none.
>
> —Adult child caregiver of Vietnam Navy veteran

Other caregivers were seeking a community of people like them and wanted providers to listen to and tailor services directly for them:

> What would be amazing is if they created a team for people that have rare chronic conditions. Once diagnosis is established and it qualifies as a rare chronic condition based upon the amount of debilitation that the patient is experiencing. Like you're referred to a program and then like a caseworker, someone starts getting involved in talking and finding out like, what do you need? What happens when you're homeless or when you get a cancer diagnosis or something like that, like there's a whole system set up. They make sure you have mental health support, and they make sure that you have a case manager to balance it all out. And then they have a nursing staff that you can talk to about any questions. I would love that for like rare chronic conditions, like once you get the diagnosis, you could be referred and then they start working with you and then provide all the resources that you need.
>
> —Partner caregiver of post-9/11-era Navy veteran

> Take the time for each individual situation to learn. It may be in the same area; we might all have the same situation, but each is different. Kind of just sit and actually sympathize and understand that specific situation.
>
> —Adult grandchild caregiver of Air Force veteran

Finally, several caregivers mentioned a desire for various types of training or additional information.

Maybe they can offer more trainings or workshops or send social workers out more often or if they hear about or know of a person having a caregiver or lack of a caregiver. . . . like information of other services that are available within the community that can be utilized. . . . Like caregiver rest days. You know, maybe they can help with like other like professional development, like, home health care certificates to people who may be wanting to be more in that field that don't have the access or even know much about that field in the community so that we can have more caregivers.

—Neighbor caregiver of veteran, unspecified service

It would be useful for me personally to have, well, like this is an example of something the hospice does well. They have, when they first take on a customer, they give you like a bag, like a grocery sack full of literature, what to expect. "This is what death looks like. These are the stages that your person is likely to go through." They have a lot of information. And for me as someone who reads a lot and studies a lot in house, advanced degrees and so forth and so on, that was fantastic. I would have loved to have had that from the cancer doctor and all of these other people providing [a] similar level of information.

—Adult child caregiver of Korean War Army veteran

CHAPTER 9

Conclusion and Recommendations

Caregiving is not a monolithic role and requires tailored solutions: Across the 38 interviews, caregivers reported a variety of positive and negative experiences in their roles. While caregivers often provided assistance with ADLs and IADLs to address care recipients' health-related conditions and needs, the challenges that they faced in doing so varied dramatically. This variability was also apparent in the types of formal and informal support, financial or other resources, and health and social services they leveraged or imagined being able to access in the future. Additionally, caregivers' perceptions of their identities, portrayals, and feelings of representation were mixed, often driven by achieved characteristics instead of by ascribed ones.

These caregivers' voices help provide additional context for the findings presented from the main report (Ramchand et al., 2024). Table 9.1 summarizes the recommendations from *Emerging from the Shadows* (Ramchand et al., 2024), highlighting which recommendations are new and which strengthened recommendations from the original 2014 report (Ramchand et al., 2014).

In the following sections, we briefly discuss how the interview findings can enrich consideration of these recommendations. The main report (Ramchand et al., 2024) contains detailed information about the current policy and service context in which those recommendations are offered.

Promote Work Environments That Are Supportive of Caregivers

The importance of work environments that are supportive of caregivers shone through in several interviews that highlighted the importance of telework and flexible schedules. In addition, several caregivers mentioned engaging in micro-entrepreneurial enterprises, such as pet grooming, to supplement their incomes. Organizations that support caregivers might explore approaches or programs to support caregivers seeking to start and operate small businesses.

TABLE 9.1

2024 Recommendations for Better Supporting Military and Veteran Caregivers

New Recommendations for 2024

Increase access to mental health and substance use treatment for caregivers and their children. In 2024, we highlight the potential value of novel mental health care delivery models—including telehealth, asynchronous counseling, mobile health apps, task shifting, and Collaborative Care (which integrates evidence-based mental health care into primary care)—to help meet the unmet mental health needs of caregivers and their children.

Increase opportunities for caregivers to access available financial support, and offer additional financial compensation to caregivers for the work they perform. We recommend that organizations that serve caregivers inform them about programs that provide financial assistance and help them apply for those programs, and we recommend that policymakers continue to explore tax credit options for caregivers.

Expand and promote home health care considering how caregivers will be affected. Caregivers may need to coordinate and train home health care teams and providers, could have increased out-of-pocket costs associated with keeping care recipients at home, and might face additional work disruptions negotiating home health care teams. Residential options should continue to be pursued and made accessible, particularly for those care recipients who will be safest in residential placement.

Focus programmatic and social support within the context of local conditions in which military/veteran caregivers live. Policies and interventions aimed at military/veteran caregivers should take local resources, such as housing, food access, or economic conditions, into account.

Strengthening Recommendations from 2014

Tailor caregiver support programs to reflect caregivers' diverse preferences and needs. We continue to recommend that organizations that serve caregivers consider the diversity in caregivers' preferences and needs in how they conduct outreach to caregivers, the content of these programs, and the ways in which programs are delivered.

Encourage health care systems to better integrate caregivers into health care teams. Health systems still need to be incentivized to better include caregivers in health care teams. Evaluation research should test whether efforts to integrate caregivers into health care environments improve patient outcomes, create cost savings, and increase demand. Policymakers should continue to consider creating new mechanisms that incentivize health care systems to integrate caregivers into health care teams.

Promote work environments that are supportive of caregivers. Although employers are increasingly offering temporal and spatial flexibility to workers, many military and veteran caregivers are not offered temporal flexibility or telework options.

Research/Evaluation Recommendations

Continue to conduct rigorous evaluations of those initiatives designed to support military and veteran caregivers. Evaluation is key to ensuring that programs are achieving their intended outcomes and are worth the resources and time that caregivers devote to participating in them.

Continue to conduct research that fully captures the breadth of caregiving and those who serve as caregivers. Defining caregivers based on the activities they perform, instead of through their identity as a caregiver, identifies many more individuals taking on caregiving roles. One research priority is to further describe these activities, particularly for caregivers to those with mental health conditions, substance use disorders, and neurocognitive conditions like TBI and dementia, to fully support caregivers to individuals with these conditions.

SOURCE: Adapted from RAND Corporation, 2024.

Increase Opportunities for Caregivers to Access Available Financial Support, and Offer Additional Financial Compensation to Caregivers for the Work They Perform

Caregivers who are retired do not need employment accommodations; rather, they may need support in navigating how to provide for both their own and their care recipients' changed financial circumstances. Income eligibility thresholds for various types of supportive services can vary considerably. Targeted guidance in navigating these complex health care and social service systems may be beneficial for some.

Furthermore, most caregivers were not actively planning for the future. Pro bono financial and legal services that help caregivers develop sustainable long-term plans for themselves and their care recipients are needed.

Encourage Health Care Systems to Better Integrate Caregivers into Health Care Teams

Efforts are underway to encourage health systems to better incorporate caregivers into care delivery teams (Elizabeth Dole Foundation, undated). Many interviewees noted with appreciation the ways in which they were successfully included and treated as valuable partners in supporting care recipients. However, quite a few noted the importance of *their own* abilities in communicating effectively with medical providers; often, those with backgrounds in health care noted this shared language or expertise as a benefit. Furthermore, efforts to enhance communication between providers and caregivers could be beneficial; these could include efforts to educate caregivers on technical terms associated with the care recipient's health-related conditions and caregiving needs and efforts to educate providers on how to better communicate technical or complex issues to caregivers.

In addition to the outreach efforts underway that target health care systems, there is a need for efforts to ensure that providers are able to competently care for patients and caregivers with diverse backgrounds and caregiving needs. This may necessitate drawing from resources on addressing implicit biases and embedding cultural responsivity in one's approach. Think Cultural Health, sponsored by the Office of Minority Health at the National Institute of Health, presents "information, continuing education opportunities, resources, and more for health and health care professionals to learn about culturally and linguistically appropriate services" (Office of Minority Health, undated).

Focus Programmatic and Social Support Within the Context of Local Conditions in Which Military/Veteran Caregivers Live

A few caregivers described geographic barriers to accessing necessary supports and services (e.g., being distally located from health care systems or services in a rural area, needing to travel to military bases to obtain health care services). Recognizing the diversity of military and veteran caregivers' identities (e.g., permanent resident versus citizen), time commitments, and potential access barriers for services, it may be helpful to raise awareness of virtual resources and services. There may also be a need to develop newer virtual models where gaps exist. Such efforts may further support those caregivers who experience difficulty in having care recipients engage in activities outside their homes.

Tailor Caregiver Support Programs to Reflect Caregivers' Diverse Preferences and Needs

Many caregivers rely on personal support networks, community organizations, and religious institutions to support their own needs and are not aware of resources specifically dedicated to serving military and veteran caregivers. Additionally, many noted that there were challenges proving eligibility for and gaining access to federal resources (e.g., VA services) available for themselves and their care recipients.

This points to potential needs to enrich outreach efforts in several ways: First, programs can enrich outreach efforts directly to caregivers, using diverse channels and mediums. Many caregivers described a lack of exposure to stories of other caregivers or did not necessarily identify with the portrayals they saw. Increasing the visibility of diverse and representative caregiver stories may further increase awareness of available resources and willingness to utilize them.

Second, programs can target other supportive organizations that are already serving caregivers in formal or informal ways to ensure that those organizations are able to direct caregivers to specific resources. For example, county-level organizations that support older adults more generally and religious organizations were regularly mentioned. Concerted outreach efforts to ensure that these programs are aware of government and nonprofit programs that support veterans and their caregivers may be beneficial.

Several caregivers expressed frustrations with the challenges involved in proving eligibility or integrating diverse types of support. Caregivers may benefit from greater awareness of and access to case managers. We take a broad approach to defining *case managers*, realizing that those fulfilling this role for caregivers can be individuals with advanced degrees in social work for those with more complex needs, and case managers can also be community health workers, peer support specialists, chaplains, or trained volunteers. Case managers can help caregivers navigate health systems and gain access to other supportive services. Veteran service organizations and other nonprofits may be able to provide critical support in helping case managers and care recipients understand and navigate eligibility processes, which can be complex. "No wrong door" systems (Bowen et al., 2017) or collective impact models (Armstrong, McDonough, and Savage, 2015) are systems-level approaches that intentionally connect community-based organizations to ensure a coordinated system of resources and referrals and could likely reduce the hassles that caregivers experience.

Conclusion

As America's hidden heroes continue to emerge from the shadows, it is critical that those who wish to support them center caregivers' voices and work to understand caregivers' diverse and nuanced experiences. These interviews offer a window into their and care recipients' challenges and needs, where and how they get support, gaps in available services, and how organizations can enhance provision of care.

Caregivers are driven by love, compassion, and duty to provide support to partners, family members, friends, and neighbors. They offer support ranging from running errands to providing skilled medical services, and the level of care they offer may change dramatically over time—particularly if their loved one's health declines. Caregivers make use of an array of formal and informal services to support themselves and their care recipients, but many are unaware of or experience challenges in accessing or navigating services. This can add to their burdens and may hinder caregivers' abilities to continue providing valuable support to our nations' veterans over the long haul, indicating ongoing opportunities for organizations wishing to support them to enhance outreach and provision of services to these hidden heroes.

APPENDIX A

Methodological Approach

Military and veteran caregivers are *hidden heroes*, a term coined by RAND and the Elizabeth Dole Foundation in 2014 when the organizations partnered to produce *Hidden Heroes: America's Military Caregivers* (Ramchand et al., 2014). That report provided the first ever national portrait of those who care—mostly uncompensated—for wounded, ill, and injured service members and veterans in the United States. *Hidden Heroes* shed light on a new class of caregivers: spouses, family members, friends, and neighbors caring for service members and veterans with wounds, illnesses, and injuries—including mental health conditions—and how caregiving disproportionately affected them.

Guided in part by the 2014 *Hidden Heroes* report, the Elizabeth Dole Foundation and others created programs and advocated for policies designed to better support military and veteran caregivers. These changes call for a new examination of military and veteran caregivers. *America's Military and Veteran Caregivers: Hidden Heroes Emerging from the Shadows* (Ramchand et al., 2024) presents this new examination of America's hidden heroes. The information in that report is derived from two sources. First, RAND researchers administered the 2023 RAND Caregiving Survey, a probabilistic survey of U.S. households that collected detailed information from caregivers and non-caregivers alike. It was designed to enumerate the number of military and veteran caregivers and further understand their needs, service utilization, and outcomes. The final analytic sample size was 2,946 respondents, including 513 military and veteran caregivers, and, for comparison, 1,205 civilian caregivers and 1,228 non-caregivers. The 2023 RAND Caregiving Survey was linked to national data characterizing where caregivers live to better understand how rural, regional, and neighborhood characteristics affect caregivers and caregiving.

To select subpopulations among military and veteran caregivers of interest for further, in-depth analysis, members of the study team considered a number of factors, including military and veteran caregiver subpopulations whose experiences seemed underrepresented in the literature (such as siblings, men, and those who identify as LGBTQ+), who seemed likely to have increased challenges accessing support and services (such as those in rural or highly rural areas and caregivers to veterans not enrolled in VA), or who were caring for veterans with health-related conditions that are disproportionately present in military populations (such as those at risk of suicide, who have PTSD, or who have catastrophic injuries). Populations extensively or recently covered in other studies (such as children) were excluded.

To focus our interviews on those who provide regular and ongoing care, we restricted interview eligibility to those caregivers who provide five or more hours of care per week. After considering input from the Scientific Advisory Board, the research team ultimately chose to focus on those caring for veterans with at least one of the following health-related conditions:

- catastrophic injuries
- depression, PTSD, and/or suicide risk
- conditions thought to result from toxic exposures
- cognitive issues/dementia.

We further restricted our sample population to caregivers in the following categories, which are underrepresented in the literature; many are not mutually exclusive:

- sibling
- not related
- man
- LGBTQ+
- Black/African American
- Hispanic
- veteran.

NORC sent a follow-up survey to 295 survey respondents who met one or more of these criteria, offering them the opportunity to participate in a telephone interview for an additional incentive. The survey was open from November 28, 2023, through December 28, 2023. NORC provided contact information for those who expressed willingness to participate to RAND on a weekly basis.

SRG then conducted follow-on outreach to those individuals. In total, SRG contacted 90 individuals who had agreed in the follow-up survey to be contacted for an interview; of these, 11 were ineligible (seven because the care recipient was never in the military and four because too much time had passed since care was provided), 32 did not respond to outreach, and seven were not interviewed (they canceled or did not show up for the interview).

Between December 12, 2023, and February 19, 2024, a team of five experienced qualitative interviewers (including two Spanish-speaking individuals) in SRG scheduled, conducted, and transcribed verbatim interviews with 40 individuals. The interviewers received project-specific training on the purpose of the interviews and the protocol before interviews began; they met intermittently to discuss any questions as interviews were conducted. Two of the interviews were conducted in Spanish by Spanish-speaking interviewers on SRG's team. One of these interviewers translated the protocol, which was then reviewed by the second Spanish-speaking interviewer. A professional translation firm translated these two interview recordings into English, which was again reviewed against the recording by the Spanish-speaking interviewer who initially translated the protocol.

The counts of the selected criteria among the 38 interviewees of the health-related conditions of the care recipient and characteristics of caregivers, as self-reported in the survey, are presented in Table A.1 and Table A.2.

Interviews ranged from 13 to 59 minutes in length, with an average length of 25 minutes. After RAND confirmed that an interview was completed, NORC provided the participant with a $40 incentive through its standard process for AmeriSpeak panelists. All research activities were approved by RAND's Human Subjects Protection Committee (RAND's Institutional Review Board).

To facilitate a rapid analysis, two of the coauthors pursued a two-stage approach. First, these two authors, who each possess qualitative research expertise, developed an abstraction matrix in Microsoft Excel based on the interview protocol. They then each abstracted four sets of randomly selected transcripts, placing relevant quotes and a summary of discussed topics in the appropriate columns of the matrix corresponding to each interview question. The authors met to discuss how they had selected key topics and illustrative quotes for each interview protocol, determining that additional modifications to their approach and the matrix were not necessary as their abstractions showed high levels of agreement; they then

TABLE A.1
Care Recipient Health-Related Conditions, as Reported by Interviewees

Care Recipient Health-Related Conditions	
Catastrophic injuries	28
Depression, PTSD, or suicide risk	20
Conditions thought to result from toxic exposures	28
Cognitive issues/dementia	16

NOTE: Most categories are not mutually exclusive.

TABLE A.2
Characteristics of Interviewed Caregivers

Self-Identified Caregiver Characteristics	
Sibling of care recipient	3
Not related to care recipient	6
Man	8
LGBTQ+	6
Black/African American	8
Hispanic	6
Veteran	5

NOTE: Most categories are not mutually exclusive.

evenly divided the remaining transcripts for abstraction. They jointly decided to exclude two interviews because, after careful consideration, the respondents appeared to be paid caregivers without a preexisting relationship to the care recipient.

Next, to conduct the thematic analysis, the columns of interview questions in the matrix were grouped into six main thematic categories: caregiver and care recipient needs; available supports; caregiver identities, portrayals, and experiences; economic impacts of caregiving; caregiver–care recipient relationships; and how organizations could improve. Each author was assigned specific thematic categories, after which an inductive approach was leveraged to identify major themes, variation within those themes, and illustrative quotes for each thematic category. The authors drafted the respective chapters for which they conducted rapid analyses of interview data, after which they reviewed one another's chapters to provide feedback. The report chapters resultingly correspond with specific questions, and themes are presented using terminology from the interview protocol and responses to best elevate caregivers' voices and experiences. The authors kept in frequent contact to ensure that any disagreements on the framing of themes and illustrative quotations were resolved. The third author then reviewed and substantively contributed to an early draft of the report, strengthening the report flow, highlighting where themes required additional explanation, and drawing connections to the survey research from which these interviewees were identified.

Interview Protocol

Thank you for taking the time to talk with us today about your experiences as a caregiver.

1. First, can you tell me the name or a nickname of the person you care for, so I can refer to them during the interview?

SCREENING QUESTIONS

I need to ask you a few quick questions, to make sure you meet the requirements for this project.

2. What is your relationship with [NAME]? (How do you know them?)

   If family member, friend, or neighbor → CONTINUE
   If aide, nurse, other medical professional, or other paid role → ask: "Do you have any relationship other than caring for him/her?"
   → *IF ALSO FRIEND, NEIGHBOR, ETC → CONTINUE*
   → *IF ONLY PAID ROLE → say:* "I am not sure if you meet the requirements for this project. I will check with my team and get back to you. If you are eligible, we will reschedule this interview. Thank you for your interest."

   NOTE: If the <u>only</u> relationship between the veteran and caregiver is a paid, formal role such as a home health aide, they are not eligible. However, it is possible for an informal caregiver such as a family member, friend, or neighbor to be paid and/or receive a stipend for their caregiving role – they would still be eligible.

3. Do you currently help care for [NAME]?

   IF YES → CONTINUE
   IF NO → ask: "How long has it been since you helped care for him/her?"
   → IF IT'S BEEN <1 MONTH → CONTINUE
   → IF IT'S BEEN 1 MONTH+ → *say:* "I am not sure if you meet the requirements for this project. I will check with my team and get back to you. If you are eligible, we will reschedule this interview. Thank you for your interest."

NOTE: The goal is to talk to current caregivers. If it has been more than a month or two since they provided care, or if the veteran has died, or if the veteran has recovered and no longer needs help – the R is not eligible.

4. Was [NAME] ever in the U.S. military?

   IF YES → CONTINUE
   IF NO → say: "I am not sure if you meet the requirements for this project. I will check with my team and get back to you. If you are eligible, we will reschedule this interview. Thank you for your interest."

   NOTE: Only caregivers of veterans who were in the U.S. Army, Navy, Air Force, Marines, Space Force, or Coast Guard, whether on active duty or in the Reserves / National Guard, are eligible for the interview. If the caregiver was in the civil service and was not in the military, the R is not eligible.

Great, thank you for answering those questions.

5. Next, can you tell me a bit about [NAME]?

   a. Why did [NAME] join the military, what did they do in the military, and how long did they serve?

   b. What condition or conditions does [NAME] have?
      i. Did that result from their military service?
      ii. When did this happen? (Do you remember appx how many years ago?)

   c. What are the things [NAME] most needs your help with?

   d. How long have you been caring for [NAME]?

6. How has being a caregiver for [NAME] changed your relationship with them?

7. What are the biggest challenges you face as a caregiver?

   IF NEEDED: These could include <u>financial issues</u>; <u>finding time to do other things</u>; <u>physical challenges</u> of caring for your loved one; <u>accessing benefits</u> your loved one is entitled to; getting <u>respite</u> from your caregiving responsibilities; <u>managing stress</u>; or trying to maintain your own <u>career</u>.

   a. Are there services you need but are unable to get?

      IF NEEDED: Services could include things like respite care, help with transportation, counseling, or training to care for [NAME].

      i. What have been the obstacles to getting those services?

8. Do you get any support to help you care for [NAME]?

   IF NEEDED:
   - *This could include in-home care, respite care, a monetary stipend, a supportive community, or anything else that you experience as support.*
   - *You could get support from friends or family, VA or other health care systems or providers, nonprofit organizations, or other caregivers.*

9. Is there anything that you think makes your experience different from other caregivers? This might include aspects of your identity / background, your relationship to [NAME], or [NAME]'s condition(s).

   a. You may hear stories about caregivers in the news, or in materials you receive from the VA, or in other places. Thinking about this - Do you feel represented in stories you see and hear about caregivers?

      i. *IF NEEDED: Do stories you see about military caregivers reflect your race, gender, sexuality, and other aspects of your identity? Why/why not?*

   b. Do you feel respected and understood by health care professionals who provide support for you and [NAME]? Why/why not?

   c. Do you feel that there are support systems or groups available for you personally? Why/why not?

   d. What could organizations do to better help you feel welcome, accepted, valued, and supported?

10. Can you tell me about how you're planning for the future?

    IF NEEDED: What changes will you need to make as you/[NAME] get older?

    a. Have you made any specific plans regarding finances, retirement, where you live, or anything else?

    b. Do you worry about your ability to continue providing care as you both age?

    c. Has your ability to continue your education, work, or save been affected by your caregiving role?

11. How has [NAME]'s condition(s) and caring for him/her affected your finances?

    a. Are you still making the same income as you did before becoming a caregiver?

    b. What types of things do you have to spend money on because of your caregiving role?

       i. Approximately how much do you spend out of pocket on these expenses?

    c. Do you receive any supplemental income from something other than a job?

12. What are the most rewarding aspects of caregiving for you?

13. Those are all of the questions I have for you today. Before we wrap up, is there anything you want to add about caregiving for [NAME] that I haven't asked about?

Thank you so much for taking the time to talk with us; your input will be invaluable for our research. Have a great day!

Abbreviations

ADL	activity of daily living
COVID-19	coronavirus disease 2019
IADL	instrumental activity of daily living
LGBTQ+	lesbian, gay, bisexual, transgender, queer, or other sexual and gender minority
PCAFC	Program of Comprehensive Assistance for Family Caregivers
PTSD	posttraumatic stress disorder
SRG	Survey Research Group
TBI	traumatic brain injury
VA	U.S. Department of Veterans Affairs

References

Armstrong, Nicholas J., James D. McDonough, Jr., and Daniel Savage, *Driving Community Impact: The Case for Local, Evidence-Based Coordination in Veteran and Military Family Services and the AmericaServes Initiative*, Syracuse University Institute for Veterans and Military Families, April 2015.

Bowen, Christina Neill, Wendy Fox-Grage, Kali Thomas, and James Rudolph, *No Wrong Door: Supporting Community Living for Veterans*, AARP Public Policy Institute, November 2017.

Elizabeth Dole Foundation, "The Campaign for Inclusive Care," webpage, undated. As of July 25, 2024:
https://www.elizabethdolefoundation.org/campaign-inclusive-care/

Office of Minority Health, "Think Cultural Health: About Us," webpage, U.S. Department of Health and Human Services, undated. As of August 14, 2024:
https://thinkculturalhealth.hhs.gov/about

Ramchand, Rajeev, Sarah Dalton, Tamara Dubowitz, Kelly Hyde, Nipher Malika, Andrew R. Morral, Elie Ohana, Vanessa Parks, Terry L. Schell, Gretchen Swabe, Thomas E. Trail, and Kayla M. Williams, *America's Military and Veteran Caregivers: Hidden Heroes Emerging from the Shadows*, RAND Corporation, RR-A3212-1, 2024. As of September 24, 2024:
https://www.rand.org/pubs/research_reports/RRA3212-1.html

Ramchand, Rajeev, Terri Tanielian, Michael P. Fisher, Christine Anne Vaughan, Thomas E. Trail, Caroline Batka, Phoenix Voorhies, Michael W. Robbins, Eric Robinson, and Bonnie Ghosh-Dastidar, *Hidden Heroes: America's Military Caregivers*, RAND Corporation, RR-499-TEDF, 2014. As of February 7, 2024:
https://www.rand.org/pubs/research_reports/RR499.html

RAND Corporation, "America's Military and Veteran Caregivers: What Has Changed from 2014 to 2024, and What Still Needs to Be Done?" RAND Corporation, RB-A3212-2, 2024. As of September 24, 2024:
https://www.rand.org/pubs/research_briefs/RBA3212-2.html

Shih, Regina A., Esther M. Friedman, Emily K. Chen, and Grace C. Whiting, "Prevalence and Correlates of Gray Market Use for Aging and Dementia Long-Term Care in the U.S.," *Journal of Applied Gerontology*, Vol. 41, No. 4, 2022.

Szymendera, Scott D., *Veterans' Benefits: Eligibility of Merchant Mariners*, Congressional Research Service, R44162, updated January 27, 2017.

U.S. Department of Veterans Affairs, *VA Benefits and Community Resources for Aging Veterans and Caregivers: Minneapolis VA Health Care System*, 2023.

RAND researchers present findings from the qualitative arm of the *America's Military and Veteran Caregivers: Hidden Heroes Emerging from the Shadows* research project, sharing insights from interviews with U.S. military and veteran caregivers. Thirty-eight qualitative interviews were conducted between December 2023 and February 2024. In the interviewed caregivers' own words, they provided rich descriptions of their experiences, complementing the main report's survey findings with illustrative anecdotes that deepen our understanding of the challenges and joys of caregiving and elucidate opportunities to improve supportive services.

Caregivers highlighted aiding care recipients with a broad array of activities of daily living and instrumental activities of daily living, often leveraging a variety of informal and formal supports. They often faced challenges, such as balancing caregiving with other priorities and commitments; managing care recipients' health-related conditions and needs; financial, emotional, and physical struggles; and difficulty accessing respite and navigating health care systems. Caregivers reflected on their identities, highlighting ways in which they are similar to and different from other caregivers; they generally said that they found caregiving to be rewarding. They also discussed the economic impacts of caregiving and pointed to opportunities for organizations to improve outreach and provision of services.

$22.00

RAND

ISBN-10 1-9774-1412-5
ISBN-13 978-1-9774-1412-0

52200

9 781977 414120

www.rand.org

Research Report

FORREST W. CRAWFORD, KYLE WEBSTER, GERALD L. EPSTEIN,
DEREK ROBERTS, JOSEPH FAIR, SELLA NEVO

Securing Commercial Nucleic Acid Synthesis

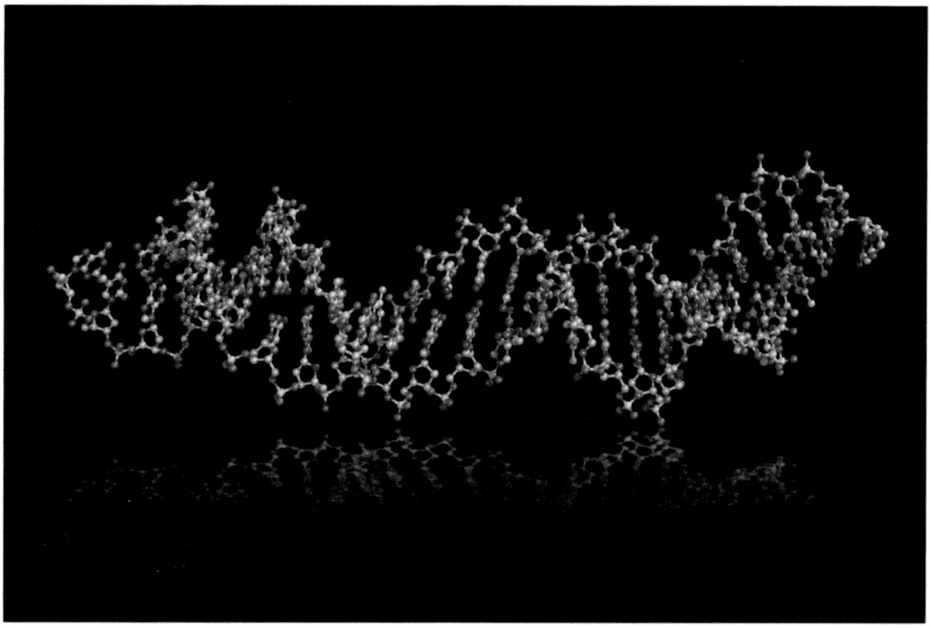